The Children's Fire

Heart Song of a People

Mac Macartney

First published in Great Britain by Practical Inspiration Publishing, 2018

ISBN 978-1-78860-045-3

 Practical Inspiration
PUBLISHING

Praise for *The Children's Fire*

'Few amongst us have both the integrity of spirit to undertake a genuine earth-walk and the poetry of soul to write about it afterwards in such passionate, powerful terms. Mac Macartney is one who has both. In this time of great turning, when we each must examine our heartfelt relationship to the earth and the more-than-human world around us, Mac's journey is a guiding light and an inspiration, a paean to the possible, to the best that we can be. With strength in the vulnerability, spanning the wide, wide spectrum of what it is to be human on this earth at this time, there could not be a more important – or timely – work.'

Manda Scott, author of the *Boudica: Dreaming* series

'Mac Macartney is a prophet of cultural renewal, an interrupter of the Western egocentric-consumer worldview, a wild man, an elder, a humble pilgrim, perhaps a present-day druid, and an enchanting storyteller. In *The Children's Fire*, he recounts his three-week solo journey on foot, without map or compass, through the scarred but still-sacred lands of his native Britain to a mythic, real, holy isle – a dreamtime pilgrimage to reclaim his/our original human wildness and belonging to the land, undertaken on behalf of the children of all species seven generations hence. You won't want to be left behind. Join him.'

Bill Plotkin, author of *Soulcraft* and *Wild Mind*

'A haunting paean to an indigenous culture that has been misrepresented for centuries, and a call for a new dedication to the Earth and all its children.'

Richard Louv, author of *The Nature Principle* and
Last Child in the Woods

'At a time when England wrestles with identity, Mac Macartney explores some origins of traumatic violence, reaching back to Roman times. Here is a pilgrim quest through geography, history and spirituality. Captivating, haunting and at times disquieting, yet: "... walking into a death landscape ... I knew that I was walking into life."'

Alastair Mcintosh, author of *Soil and Soul* and
Poacher's Pilgrimage

'When Mac Macartney speaks, you listen. His is a true and, sadly, rare voice of wisdom in our times. His words come from a place of 'embodied' knowing, rather than the all-too-common preachings of the conceptual mind. His written words resonate with the same depth of wisdom and, if you let them in, will nourish your very core. Our minds may have become adept at dismissing wisdom, but our hearts know what really makes sense. Mac writes to your heart – listen to him and to it.'

Bruce Parry, documentary maker

'If, like me, you are baffled by how it's possible for humanity to throw itself headlong, in the face of overwhelming evidence, down a path that is impoverishing our environment then this book hints at an intriguing possibility. Honest and soul-bearing, *The Children's Fire* is an account of one man's journey, unaided and on foot, following an ancient path through landscape and history to reveal a rich vein of British indigenous culture. Like so many indigenous cultures around the world, the tribes of

Britain lived in concert with, and at the mercy of, nature's rhythms. And, like so many indigenous cultures, their demise was marked by a brutal invasion that left a deep collective trauma and disconnect. *The Children's Fire* makes the bold suggestion that this trauma more than ripples on today – it is firmly in the driving seat of our dysfunctional relationship with the natural world. A fascinating re-framing of Britain's ancient history that offers a fresh perspective to a very modern question of whether it's possible to live our twenty-first-century lives in harmony with the natural world.'

Gillian Burke, biologist and broadcaster

'Do not be deceived by the beautiful lyricism of *The Children's Fire*. Beneath the evocative and multi-layered description of Mac's wintertime pilgrimage from Malvern to Anglesey lies a hard-hitting commentary on contemporary society, emphasising the existential threat inherent in our present direction, and the vital need to shift from "dominion over" to "relationship with". Highly recommended.'

Roz Savage, author, speaker, ocean rower

'I have often lamented the seeming European lack of in-touchness with indigenous traditions – but this book forcefully erases that lament. Operating from a dictate by a Native American elder to make contact with the seemingly "lost" indigenous soul of his own land, the author moves courageously in both theory and practice to heal the soul loss. Theoretically, he makes a strong case for the imperial conquest of Rome having not only wiped out the ancient wisdom and cultures, but even the appreciation of these cultures, and he sees that same imperial energy operating during 2000 years of Western history. In practice, he dares to undergo his own rite of passage by embarking on an adventurous pilgrimage on ancient trails in the depths of a severe winter to arrive at a holy place of his Celtic ancestors. The result is a magical, spiritual, political tour de force – a trumpet blast that pierces the spiritual somnolence of ages, that England is back and it is the ancient respect for the sacredness of creation that will retire human anthropocentrism and its accompanying imperialism and will awaken Europe again. Creation spirituality indeed!'

Matthew Fox, author of *Original Blessing*

'The Children's Fire is a roadmap for our species. Charted by a remarkable explorer who has made this journey himself, it takes us deep into forests and places of wildness, and into the heart of "incorruptible sanity". It steers us back from the brink of planetary extinction.'

Richard Reoch, former President of Shambhala, the global community based on the Buddha's teachings on Enlightened Society

'Mac Macartney inspires me. He is an important guide for our time. In *The Children's Fire*, he invites us into a deepening of life and love of life. He describes a sacred purpose we can all share and take part in – to mend what is broken – contributing to the recovery of our world and ourselves.'

Chris Johnstone, co-author of *Active Hope – how to face the mess we're in without going crazy*

'I love Mac's book. Here's a glimpse of a journey of a man choosing the high road – as he treks, he travels deep into his innermost being and steps out of his comfort zone. And what an odyssey – one that had me living and breathing with Mac, every step he takes. *The Children's Fire* shall burn deeply into all our hearts.'

Polly Higgins, Ecocide law pioneer, award-winning author and barrister

To my wife, Wandia, and my two sons, Kevo and Cai, for giving me a home.

In testimony to all indigenous peoples who have stood in dignified truth against the harsh disinterest of a system that counts nothing of value which does not fit inside an accountant's ledger.

Contents

Maps

Biography

MAC MACARTNEY IS the founder of Embercombe, a social enterprise dedicated to deepening our connection with nature and inspiring people from all walks of life to bravely contribute towards a world that honours the Children's Fire. He was also the founder and CEO of a leadership consultancy for corporate executives, operating internationally between 1989 and 2005.

Over a period of twenty years, Mac was mentored and coached by a group of Native American teachers. During this training and ever since, he has attempted to bring two worlds together – an ancient worldview that emphasises relationship, interdependence and reverence for life with the huge challenges and equally huge opportunities of the twenty-first century.

Mac is an international speaker on topics such as responsible leadership, sustainability, spirituality and indigenous wisdom. Presentations to business organisations include the Mars Corporation, Unilever and BP. He also sits on the advisory board for Danone North America. Mac speaks regularly at many festivals, including Glastonbury, Wilderness, Buddhafield, Shambala, Port Elliot, and numerous conferences and events both in the UK and abroad. He has spoken at four TEDx events.

Mac holds a Bachelor's degree in Education and a Master's degree in Human Resource Development, and was awarded an Honorary Doctorate by the University of Plymouth in 2015. In 2013 he was awarded the Enlightened Society Award by Sakyong Mipham Rinpoche.

Mac lives in Devon with his wife and two sons. You can find out more at www.macmacartney.com.

Acknowledgements

THE JOURNEY AROUND which this book twines itself was often difficult and often joyful, as indeed was the writing of it, but far more challenging has been the process of bringing it to publication. To hold faith in the work and in my ability as a writer would not have been possible without the friendship, expertise and unqualified support of some very special people.

In particular, I wish to thank Lorna Howarth of the Write Factor. Her generosity, encouragement and advice could not have come at a better time and, although she may not have realised it, she helped me through a particularly low period.

I am deeply appreciative to Alison Jones of Practical Inspiration Publishing and the friendly, professional, transparent and expert service that she, and her colleagues, have provided in bringing this book to publication.

Holly Clifton Brown graciously undertook the illustrations, and produced some very captivating work for which I am deeply grateful, and for much of the time during which the manuscript was written, Rosa Sommer Martin was a great ally to me in her positive, organised management of my work as well as standing next to me as I negotiated the rough-and-tumble of juggling time, money, energy and life in general.

I am also very appreciative of Valerie Thome, who undertook a key role of supporting me during the journey itself and whose diligence in this respect also provided me with the means to reflect on the route that I had taken once safely home.

There are many others who, in one way or another, assisted me in this work. In particular, I offer my heartfelt gratitude to Charles Anderson, Joey Waterson, Jonathan Snell, Carole Catto, David Mann, Giles Hutchins, Rachel Fleming, Mel Trievnor, Eric Maddern, Sheila Brook, Mark Thomas, Sam Robinson, Nina Farr, Paula Good and Michael Mann.

Lastly, a big 'thank you' to Jon Young, who generously, and immediately, accepted my invitation to write the Foreword to this book. Together with Lorna Howarth, his feedback also led to the Children's Fire becoming central to the book's narrative and invitation.

Foreword

M AC MACARTNEY IS an exemplary village builder and elder. His journey, part of which Mac shares through *The Children's Fire: Heart Song of a People*, is a journey to gather and share the elements of culture that will nourish the soils of restoration for all of us sharing this amazing, delicate and rare planet. At one point in Mac's journey, his elder and mentor instructs him:

> Mend what was broken. Rekindle the Children's Fire.

Four decades ago, I began to walk a path researching how people connect with themselves, with one another and with the natural world around them. This has taken me to visit many individuals, places, communities, families and organisations around the world. The relationships that I gratefully tend through my vocation are with people who are also actively working to 'mend what was broken'. My efforts often centre around supporting the designing, building and facilitating of new social patterns that bring about connection with nature, with self and with other people.

Wherever I go there are people who are interested in a positive path forward, in spite of the challenging circumstances facing them. Together we look at various ways to improve the quality of their personal lives, the lives of others around them and usually, especially, the lives of children. We look at the restoration of the invisible structures that guide and hold us as people – in other words, we look at culture. Some aspects of culture support us; these are the positive ones. Some aspects of culture entrap and oppress us; these are the ones we seek to influence for the better.

We call this work 'village building', or 'culture repair'. There are artisans of culture repair all over our planet right now. Their primary mission is to make life better and all of them know that this has to move forward to the benefit of future generations.

'Culture' is a word with an elusive meaning; it's not a topic we grapple with easily. Mac's story of the Children's Fire also reveals the invisible threads of the legacy of history that either support us or wear us down. Whenever we endeavor in having a more active role as designers and facilitators of cultural change, we must face headlong the truth of hidden history.

Decades ago, a wise Elder once shared with me that, 'in order to move forward in a better way, we have to know exactly where we have been.' He was talking to me about the truth of history that his culture and people suffered from – and continue to suffer from to this day. His, an indigenous culture, was conquered and enslaved by an invading culture with a powerful army and oppressive social structures. I don't really need to name his specific tribe, or moment in history, because everywhere I go on the planet the story is so similar – in many places there have been successive waves and layers of conquest over centuries leaving their scars and influences in a nearly invisible matrix now called 'normal'.

The story of civilisation spreading around the world needs to be retold more honestly. Those who dare to influence culture towards positive and more connective outcomes are only able to do so once they have looked directly in the eye of the historical trauma story of their place, their people, their neighbours, their environments and, ultimately, in themselves.

When we fully acknowledge where we have been, and what has happened, in enough detail to feel the patterns of influence, then we can begin the task of designing and building a better now and a better future. In walking the invisible path, Mac Macartney shares a story with a detective's skill in revealing the layers and levels of influences generating our current 'reality'. Mac represents a true role model for what's possible and ties the threads of hope in the act of commitment of mending what is broken, planting seeds for the future and rekindling the children's fire.

Jon Young, tracker, naturalist, cultural specialist; author of *What The Robin Knows* and *Coyote's Guide to Connecting with Nature*; founder of 8 Shields and the Wilderness Awareness School

An Invitation to the Reader from Two Native American Friends

We met Mac while in Australia a few years ago. Mac's energy, ease with himself, his intense personal power and disarming demeanour won our hearts immediately, and we saw him as a brother and uncle. We thought, 'here is a man who knows the heart of the earth and, as a result, his own.' We also feel that here is a man who has made the journey to peel back the layers of trauma accumulated over a lifetime and rediscover his deeper self; a man who has then tested and challenged himself not only in the physical world, but in the emotional, mental and spiritual realms – and come out alive. This life journey has proven to be amazing for Mac, as it is indeed for each and every one of us who in our own way discovers the work we are meant to do in this life.

These journeys can best be done with the widest, most inclusive and most varied perspective possible. In this way we can offer the world, each other and ourselves what we truly need. Love. None of us can do this alone. We all need the honest, compassionate reflection of ourselves to be fed back to us by those we trust and love in order to be our most open and vulnerable. We have never been, are not now, nor ever will be, alone. We stand on the shoulders of our ancestors. They are the reason we exist today. We stand at the door waiting and planning for those not yet here, those faces of the unborn yet to come. They, too, are the reason we exist today.

So let us walk together. Find that part of you that can witness your circumstances without judgement, that can consider the future while remaining in the present, that can learn from and heal the past while walking through the world that we create with every thought, word and deed. In this way we will become the soil upon which our families and all others will one day walk.

All people in all cultures hold the key to the future through following the path set by their ancestors. The tracks may be faint, the memory unspoken and encouragement hard to come by, but the path will always remain available to those who search. This way we will find our way home and leave an enriched, continuing legacy to nourish the future of all peoples – to the next seven generations and beyond.

Loretta 'Afraid-of-Bear' Cook (Lakota elder, grandmother, co-leader for the Afraid-of-Bear/American Horse Sundance) and Karonhiénhawe Linda Delormier (Mohawk, Snipe Clan)

Preface

Defeat, my Defeat, my bold companion,
You shall hear my songs and my cries and my silences,
And none but you shall speak to me of the beating of wings,
And urging of seas,
And of mountains that burn in the night,
And you alone shall climb my steep and rocky soul.

Defeat, my Defeat, my deathless courage,
You and I shall laugh together with the storm,
And together we shall dig graves for all that die in us,
And we shall stand in the sun with a will,
And we shall be dangerous.

Extract from *Defeat* by Kahlil Gibran

IN 60 CE, Gaius Suetonius Paulinus, Roman Governor of Britain, assembled the Legio XIV Gemina and a further company of veterans from the XX Legion. Along with specialist auxiliary units, he brought his army to the shores of the Menai Straits, looking across to the holy Isle of Anglesey, or Mona, as it was then. Mona was the last stronghold of the druids, and the beating heart of resistance to Rome and all it stood for. Ranged against the Roman Army on the opposite shore were thousands of Celtic warriors, druids and people from diverse British tribes, but once across the water the conflict's outcome was inevitable. It was a bloodbath; no quarter was shown. Many, including women and children, were thrown alive into the burning pyres that had once been sacred groves. The killing was methodical, absolute and without mercy.

As the slaughter on Mona continued, word came of an uprising in the east. Led by the Iceni chieftain, Boudica, a loose coalition of tribes was on the move and posing a serious threat to the Roman occupation. Suetonius Paulinus abruptly left Mona and, later in the year, a decisive battle was fought at an unknown site in the midlands of Britain. While Mona stood there was hope, and the people could still dream of freedom. When the sacred groves of Britain's ancient spiritual tradition were cut and burned, and Boudica's army was defeated by the legions, a cord was severed that has never fully healed. I believe that we learned something in this period of history that seared itself into our very soul and, like the abused child, we grew to adulthood and exported our trauma around the world. It took an unprecedented order of brutality to shock Rome, but Suetonius Paulinus achieved this with some ease. Later in the same year, while engaged in 'mopping up' operations after the battle with Boudica's army, he allowed his vengeful zeal free rein. After the intercession of the Roman Procurator of Britain, who feared that the excesses of the general might provoke further rebellion, Emperor Nero recalled Paulinus to Rome, and relieved him of his British command. It had been reported, and proven, that his interpretation of 'justice' knew no bounds.

Gaius Suetonius Paulinus is with us still.

Suetonius Paulinus lives on in our market economy, our compromised social values, the self-loathing that is evident in a culture that sets profit above wellbeing, our fear of beauty and commitment and our unwillingness to stand for the future happiness of our children. Even the itinerant Galilean rabbi Jesus of Nazareth, whose ministry unequivocally spoke of love, compassion and peace, was eventually adopted by Rome and, over the centuries, his message has been carefully manipulated to serve the ravenous hunger of various empires seeking to justify their quest for power, influence and wealth. The cost to humans and non-humans alike has been enormous. And still it goes on. Thousands of innocent lives, howling in despair, as their demise is judged to be worth the accrual of fame and fortune. Five centuries after the death of Jesus, Saint Patrick, the Romano-Christian missionary and bishop in Ireland, declared:

> I invoke today all these virtues against every hostile merciless power ... Against the spells of women, and smiths, and druids, against every knowledge that binds the soul of man.

Women, smiths and druids. He might as well have said: 'All those difficult to enslave and control; all those with access to truths that might set people free; all those of whom we are frightened.' Christianity, together with the majority of world religions and secular ideologies that have had aspirations to greatness at one time or another, have gone the same way, often many times – the secular at least as cruel as the religious. In many cases the problem has not been with the visionary, but rather with the church or government that he, and occasionally she, has had created in their name. We are alive at a time when this story, endlessly repeated by humans of all kinds, is coming home to roost. It seems we are enslaved to a worldview that will see our hopes and dreams choke to death, in the profligacy and squalor of stories and beliefs that serve the few, while harming the many. Yet, for the most part, we co-operate and give obeisance to a notion of civilisation we should have rejected long ago.

> None are more hopelessly enslaved than those who falsely believe they are free.[1]

One thousand nine hundred and forty-nine years after these events, a man in his late middle age walked a pathway to Mona

---

[1] Johann Wolfgang von Goethe Bk. II, Ch. 5; source: Die Wahlverwandtschaften, Hamburger Ausgabe, Bd. 6 (Romane und Novellen I), dtv Verlag, München, 1982, p. 397 (II.5)

again. Mentored and trained by Native American teachers and the felt embrace of an awakening zeitgeist, he dreamed of a time when we would call our land sacred once more, when the hoop of our people would be joined and we would remember our true purpose. As the 'elder brother' Kogi Indians of the High Sierras say:

To care for all living things.

I am that man.

We can no longer simply hope for a happy outcome. Some would say that we have crossed the Rubicon and now travel in the darkening maw of indifference, among the ruins of possibilities that have succumbed to societal amnesia. I, and increasingly others, say we have to go beyond hope and *choose life*, expressing this in *action*. We long to come home and, while babies are still born and stories are told that lighten the soul, fire the imagination and stir the remembering of our deep dreaming, I will delight in this life. I will thank creation for the opportunity to leverage the privilege that others have won on my behalf, and strongly bid for freedoms still imprisoned in the cultural mind of a deceased Roman general of the first century CE.

CORNOVII

DECEANGLI

THE SACRED OAK GROVES
MONA

BRYN CELLI DDU

BRYN CELLI DDU BURIAL CHAMBER

THE BRIDGE ROUNDHOUSE

GANGANI

SNOWDONIA

LLYN TEGID

ORDOVICES

CAMBRIAN MOUNTAINS

BRITISH CAMP
IRON AGE HILLFORT
MALVERN HILLS
★ STARTING POINT

DEMETAE

BRECON BEACONS

BLACK MOUNTAINS

SILURES

JOURNEY LAND

KNIFE CEREMONY
EMBERCOMBE
DEVON

Map 1

Chapter 1
The Children's Fire

A community not built around children is no community at all.[2]

WE LEAD STRANGE and discombobulated lives. Somehow, the bits do not seem to be properly connected, in relationship or integrated within a larger coherent whole. It seems that many of us live with an uneasy feeling that we are not quite where we should be, without necessarily knowing precisely where that place is. We are more comfortable than any generation before us, yet we do not seem to be happier, and in almost every sphere of life uncertainty, insecurity and anxiety tend to prevail. We work uncommonly hard just to pay our monthly bills and the notion of a 'job for life' is scarcely remembered. For many of our young people a 'job at all' would be appreciated. The sophistication of our technology grows apace, and we spend ever more hours staring at screens, living somebody else's life as our bodies soften, swell and spread. We look for fulfilment

---

[2] George Monbiot, 'Children in our towns and cities are being robbed of safe places to play', 6 January 2015. www.theguardian.com/commentisfree/2015/jan/06/children-towns-and-cities-robbed-spaces-play and www.monbiot.com/2015/01/06/the-child-inside/.

in relationships and are mostly disappointed. We have lots of information, but precious little understanding.

It is not encouraging; yet push beneath the surface, scout around a little, and it will not take long before we scent a new trail, a new story and the first stanzas of a new song.

I love journeys. I love the ideas and evocative images conjured by the word, journey. While I have breath, I always wish to journey. It is not quite the same as travelling and even though my experience of such in recent years has been of one rather narrow genre, travel is still not properly descriptive of this thing called 'journey', which brings me such unbridled feelings of engagement and fulfilment.

Over the last few years, I have enjoyed travelling and visiting many parts of our world as part of my work, influencing business towards values and practices that will serve our Earth and people better. Too many times, however, I have loitered in plush hotels, become lost in vast corporate offices, sat motionless in traffic jams of monumental proportions or sat with my head in my hands, attempting to assess whether the value of my work justifies *just one more* air flight. I have struggled with numerous concierges, intent on taking my bag when this last, pathetic act of independence was all that my fragile self-respect retained. I have arrived in rooms that cost half a month's salary, and repeatedly failed to master the array of technology that promises so much, yet yields so very little. I have struggled with destructive childish impulses when failing to fathom the chic and stylish dials that tempt me with a hot bath or a steaming shower, and I have written notes pleading with the chambermaid not to change my sheets again. I have provided feedback to hotel managers that their obsequious messages about replacing towels and caring for the environment threaten to invoke a depth of primal rage in me that might go badly for all of us. On countless occasions I have been reassured that my internet connection is functioning normally, before then spending a long, jet-lagged evening proving them wrong. I have entered innumerable corporate atriums, gawped at the carefully contrived, flawless, chilled beauty of the receptionist, entertained security staff trying to apply my electronic key and then, thankfully, found refuge in the men's rest room. Here, on two separate occasions, I have briefly meditated at the urinal and then turned to the basins to wash my hands. I have spun the taps and dipped my hands, mentally preparing myself for the meeting ahead. With scarcely a gurgle, the taps have delivered a cataract of water that has exploded from the tap, ricocheted off the white porcelain and, exactly parallel to the floor, delivered a litre of scalding water to my crotch before I have had time to turn them off again. I have endured such indignities and, biting my lip, have haltingly explained the whole unlikely story to executives for whom things like this never seem to happen. I have done all of this and, to my knowledge, it has not brought me any closer to anybody or anything – except, perhaps, the limits of my endurance. I now announce myself to be a free man and provide this book as evidence of my latest attempt to speak true.

This book, like the first, is about a journey – one that squeezed, stretched and shook me like a worm in the beak of a blackbird; an enquiry that led me farther along a pathway that had been revealed to me in the scorching sunburnt mystery of a tree-dance ceremony. In 2009, I walked an invisible path deep into the bewildered land of my own country. Along the way I was frozen with cold, retching my stomach contents before disinterested observers, lost, found and, on one very dark night, as lonely as I have never been, before or since. I deployed everything that I have learned and everything that I have within me to burrow my way into this old, secretive, wild and sacred land of Britain. I had the most intense experiences, both beautiful and profane. Homo Necans, 'man the killer', stalked my tracks, yet I also felt many prolonged moments of deep peace. The people I met were a revelation, and if I needed any experience to inform or remind myself of how generous, compassionate, warm and hospitable most people are when encountering a stranger, then this certainly pierced my heart. It was a mythic path that I walked. I was the bucket thrown into the depths of an ancient well; I found water, and it was clean and good. In our ignorance, we gave 'myth' a new and negative meaning, but in truth we need myths that will take us close to the Earth again, and to the great furnace from which all genuine spiritual experience is generated. This way, we will find ourselves, be able to set our compass and walk back towards our hearts, which we left bleeding and forgotten by a landfill site in some time past. Contrary to popular belief, our pagan ancestors did not worship the sun, rivers, stars or trees. They saw, in nature, the animate reflection of an unknowable spiritual power that sang to their humanity and helped them to understand that they were the children of creation and owed everything to this power. In the form of rocks, dreams, caves and eclipses, our wisest ancestors saw the living language of creation, and intuitively responded with reverence. In the mystery of the feminine and masculine they knelt, awed by multi-faceted energy streams that dwarfed their human intellects. Our ancient family of grandmothers and grandfathers were sophisticated people and do not deserve our patronising and embarrassing condescension. They correctly perceived the capacity humans have for hubris and the devastating, corrupting effect that power has on most of us. All of this was incorporated into myths, ceremonies and a worldview that strove to teach wisdom. So much that was once known is in that landfill.

Years past, during one of the visits to my Native American teachers, on a very cold and frosty night, for a brief moment I saw the immensity of space and simultaneously experienced my colossal incapacity to comprehend the truly big. My mentors shared a fragment of this wisdom with me; I was led along a path that slowly contoured a small wooded hill to a fire. I could see the flames darting, curving, spiralling, offering thousands of tiny suns to the unknown darkness beyond and the graceful, dancing arms of the pine trees waving them on their way. That night I felt animal; I could feel blood heat surging in the canyons of my body. My torso heaved with power and my arms remembered the weight of hefting a weapon. As I drew closer to the smoke-obscured forms of people waiting to receive me, I felt close and intimate with bear and wolf, hare and falcon. I knew I had the capacity to terrify, the inclination to protect, the depth to howl, as humans once knew how.

Sit here, Mac. We wish to speak with you about something important.

It was on this occasion that I first heard about the Children's Fire. Some hundreds of years ago, chiefs – women and men – sat in council. They pondered the question, 'How shall we govern our people?' I see the circle of chiefs now, in this moment. I see them rise and turn to face the wild country around them. Abruptly, the circle widens as they walk their silent, solitary and prayerful steps outwards into the folding land. Trained to listen to the Earth Mother, breathing with the wind, seeing with the sun and feeling with the waters, barefoot to the earth. 'How shall we govern our people?'

The chiefs did what they would always do. They felt into the profound mystery of the world around them and, knowing themselves as relatives to everything in existence, they knew their question would be answered. That it would be revealed in the teaching circle of creation, alive and present everywhere.

How long did they listen? How many times did the circle shrink and widen as insights were shared, contemplated and held in dialogue? Like Gautama Buddha as he sat under the Bodhi Tree, or the Prophet Mohammed in his cave, or Moses on the mountain, or Jesus in the desert, the chiefs went to nature for guidance. Respectful, trusting, exercising presence, softening, alert and awake. Let us imagine that, at the conclusion of this enquiry, when all had been said and the chiefs were soon to return to the village, one of the grandmothers spoke, summarising her understanding of the wisdom that had been given to them.

We have listened, spoken and found our way to some new understandings. The question we ask will remain alive, yielding insights that will grow and deepen as we do likewise.

This, however, will remain constant, a pledge to our people and to life. Each time we gather in council we will build a small fire in the centre of our circle of chiefs. The Children's Fire. This fire will be a living reminder of our pledge to hold the children in our hearts as we create and break laws, settle disputes and lead our people. No law, no decision, no commitment, no action, nothing of any kind will be permitted to go forth from this council that will harm the children, now or ever.

I wonder at the silence that followed these words. The silence that descended upon the chiefs as the full weight and significance of this pledge settled and became known to them.

nothing of any kind will be permitted to go forth from this council that will harm the children… now or ever.

The children – who are the children? The myopic, cultural mind we usually deploy tends towards the obvious and the convenient. At full stretch and assuming no troublesome trade disputes, squabbles over territory, irksome cultural differences or covert jealousies, theoretically (and with certain caveats), we might extend our generosity to include all human children. This does not even approach the depth, insight and compassion of the Children's Fire pledge. 'The children' included the young of all kind, the loved and universally vulnerable babies and youth of all life forms. In this way, the council chief's pledge stated the startling truth of our species' soul-knowing: that we have a duty of care to all living things. The indigenous people from whom this wisdom emerged were not troubled by the paradox of their reliance on certain animals to provide them with food, clothing, tools and shelter. All life feeds and depends upon other life forms, and the health of many species is predicated upon the attention of those who hunt. 'Harm' was understood in the context of taking what was needed but no more, of valuing the gift that another's death provides and assuming love and gratitude as the only appropriate mindset for the hunter. Relatively recent archaeological research has shown us that our very ancient indigenous ancestors may not have been so careful in their harvesting of Earth's bounty. Every continent on Earth was once populated by mega-fauna, now extinct, and the reason for its worldwide demise was human. It seems we walked into Eden, and with the assistance of our prodigious and ever-increasing capacity to think and wield tools, we assumed that, without restraint, the cornucopia of food was ours for the taking. The ancestors of many indigenous peoples around the world acquired wisdom in the ways known to all youth. They made mistakes. Deep in the culture, myths and practice of most remaining indigenous people is the knowledge that we prosper through collaboration, empathy and careful attention to the subtle delicacy of the interdependent web of living, in which all is encompassed and has a seat at the table. It is an abundant world, generous beyond measure and a most wondrous place to learn and grow, to journey.

There is a simplicity and elegance to this pledge that cuts across our practised cynicism.

In the days that followed, I had plenty of opportunity to reflect upon the yawning, shameful gap that separated my people and society from that which gave birth to the Children's Fire. The days passed, and I spent many hours assisting with a variety of tasks associated with the daily routine of the community. The work allowed me space and time to think and feel. Although I loved the mountains and pine-forested slopes of this land, my mind kept drifting back to Britain and I slowly became ever more aware of a surging, aching, atavistic sense of loss. I became aware of the grief that accompanies the sense of not belonging, of having no family, no rootedness, no memory of wild land, wild people and wild ways. Sat by other fires over the weeks that followed, I heard it suggested that my own people once knew that their land was sacred. It was suggested to me that something similar to the Children's Fire might have existed at one time in Britain. That the tribes living in pre-Roman Britain were unlikely to be the primitive, faintly ridiculous, uncouth caricatures that our

Christian-Roman history had taught us; that there was evidence to suggest a highly sophisticated tribal people who had evolved equally sophisticated ceremonies, and whose understanding of the natural world was both profound and subtle. That to assume my ancestors were ignorant, barbaric yobs on the basis of a few random, fragmented accounts, written by a clutch of highly politicised Roman commentators, was unwise. That if we were determined to locate this harsh, uncompromising story, then perhaps we should look a little closer to home and closer to this time.

Our stone circles, the standing stones, the burial mounds, the oak groves that were cut down, even the very land itself, all speak of stories untold for hundreds and hundreds of years. Stories of a time when we still occupied a world that spoke to us in the fleeting, subtle language of intuition and dreams; when we valued each other and the living, breathing, pulsing land, more than the coin sat heavy in our pocket, inert, awaiting the next transaction. Human beings are 'journeyers'. We hunger for adventure and will never satiate our desire to explore, understand and probe further. The questions that beg asking relate to the vision and principles that will guide that exploring, not the exploring itself. As we blunder into new realms of opportunity, wide-eyed and breathless at the delights promised by artificial intelligence – secretly convinced that we are gods and that being capable of doing something is sufficient reason to do it – we abdicate our soul purpose and become even more lost and lonely.

There was no past golden age, neither in Britain nor anywhere else, and the tribal people of this land were never more than the complex, contradictory, gifted and diverse people that they are now; but also, just like now, we held the keys to great banks of knowledge and insight. Much of that knowledge and insight has been lost, including perhaps that, in this final hour, we could reassert the pledge of the Children's Fire. One crucial piece of knowledge that we held and later lost is, however, of pre-eminent significance. It is this that we must reclaim. We lost the knowledge, not the belief; the knowledge that life exists in the smallest nondescript stone, in the muddy slow-flowing stream, in the animals and plants that provide us with their bodies, in the great winds that, high above us, race with the gods. We lost the capacity to revere and we lost our sense of sacredness. In a way, we lost trust. Just like the young human pushing against the limits of parenting, we stormed out the door and slammed it behind us. We are still registered on the list of missing persons and, back at home, grief still persists among our siblings – even if our parents, seeing into the well of all things past and yet to be, remain hopeful of our sheepish return.

When we left home, we had to construct a story that would both absolve us of blame and ridicule the past. A new story was required that permitted the extravagances we eagerly anticipated. That story declared war on nature, never understanding that we, too, are included in that great power. It was a bid for divinity; a snatch at the heavens. It has cost us dear, but even more so our relatives.

Faithkeeper of the Turtle Clan of the Onondaga Nation, Chief Oren Lyons, speaks of his people's prophecies.

> We were told that you could tell the extent of the degradation of the Earth because there would be two very important systems to warn you.
>
> One would be the acceleration of the winds. We were told that the winds would accelerate and continue to accelerate. When you see that the acceleration of the winds is growing, then you are in dangerous times. They said the other way to tell that the Earth was in degradation was how people treated their children. They said it will be very important to note how people treat their children, and that will tell you how the Earth is degrading. So when you open up the newspapers today, they talk about exploitative sex and children, they talk about homeless children, and you can

count homeless children by the millions. To us, it is a severe indication of the degradation. Society doesn't care.[3]

A society that does not care is a society lost to itself, an insane society. It would be as if when our chiefs radiated away from the council circle, one or two of them became distracted and never returned. The integrity of the circle now compromised, other chiefs forget their pledge and, in time, the whole council dissolves. Alone, in the wild land of our imagining, a small fire burns untended. Only the bent, compressed grass attests to the memory of chiefs who once knew their responsibilities and accepted the challenge of eldership. In the distance, we can see the stooped backs of council chiefs wandering homeward on paths that have no purpose, sheep tracks that fade and merge. Without prayerful attention, the fire becomes vague and unfocused. It loses power and soon the last flame gives itself back to the sun. Now, just smoke; now dust; now, a bare patch upon the ground; now nothing; only a memory that, borne on the wind, seeks to access the dreams of a sleeping beauty awaiting her prince's kiss.

The Children's Fire is, of course, not only a pledge to the love and welfare of the young. It is a paean to life and the promise of a continuing future; it is an assertion of confidence, an affirmation; it declares a people's fitness to take a seat at the table and, along with all other life forms, sings the anthem of belonging. When the Children's Fire is neglected we are asked two questions: 'Is our story complete? Is it time to go now?' If we answer, 'not yet', then the third question is: 'What is required of us that we may find our way to a renewal?'

So, this is our journey. The oft-repeated idiom of not being able to see the wood for the trees is generally understood as an observation of our tendency to become caught up in detail and our failure to see the important larger truth. I have found myself

---

[3] Chief Oren Lyons, 'Listening to Natural Law', in *Spiritual Ecology: The Cry of the Earth*, ed. Llewellyn Vaughan-Lee, The Golden Sufi Center, 2014, p. 7. https://goldensufi.org/book_desc_s_ecology.html.

interpreting it in a different way. With stringent clarity, this little homespun wisdom admonishes us, stating that value is with the timber, not with the tree itself. It advises us to look past the tree to the superior importance of the products it can provide us with. It tells us that our judgment is clouded and obscured by the irrelevance of the tree. If ever there was a truism it must be that we 'fail to see the trees for the wood'.

In the summer of 2008, I planned a journey that would take me to the trees; I was homeward bound.

Located on Britain's western shore and sharing a 160-mile-long border with England is the land of Wales. In the northwest corner of Wales is the island of Ynys Môn, better known to many as Anglesey. The island is approximately twenty-two miles in diameter and is separated from the mainland by a very beautiful, but notoriously dangerous, stretch of water called the Menai Straits. Once a formidable natural defence, the fast-flowing tides that surge between the island and the mainland no longer inconvenience the flow of visitors. In recent times, this island has hosted an aluminium smelting plant, a copper mining operation, a nuclear power station and a bromine extraction plant. The RAF has a base from where fast-jet pilots are trained, and the numerous sandy beaches attract more than two million visitors each year.

Inconspicuous among the fields and hedgerows of this mostly low-lying island are 143 scheduled monuments, attesting to 4000 years of mostly long-forgotten human history, with sites including hillforts, hut circles, standing stones, tombs and burial chambers. Two thousand years ago the Romans knew this island by the name of 'Mona'. As the etymology of this ancient name remains a mystery, we do not know whether the indigenous people living on and around the island knew it by the same name, but it is, of course, possible. I like the name, as it is redolent of an earth goddess, the moon and mother, and because I have good reason to deeply respect the ancient living memory of this place, which I experience as sacred. There are some who believe that the powerful dreaming of Mona's pre-Christian past has long since shrunk back into the penumbra of lost knowledge and significance. I do not think that this is true.

We were a small group of friends who shared a sense of the rising eco-spiritual zeitgeist that was emerging from the ashes of the failed flower-power movement. It was a fragile alliance, but nonetheless resolute and, in my case at least, the container within which the first murmurings of an embryonic social conscience found purchase. In the late '70s and early '80s, we had become aware of Sir George Trevelyan; tall, with a shock of resplendent white hair, a gifted orator and, brimming with the vision of a coming new age, he was like some kind of latter-day St John the Baptist. Occasionally startled by his rhetoric and, hovering on the edge of disbelief, I was nonetheless captivated by his love of life, and brave advocacy of what might yet be possible. Nascent, unformed images of a purpose-impregnated life were again taking shape in my imagination, and George was living proof that ideals did not have to capitulate to age. He articulated a vision for us and we felt the resonance in our own hearts. At a delicate and crucial time, he signposted the way towards a coherent, integrated, spirit-infused life that, I sensed, might be a place I could call home.

With George Trevelyan's ringing invitation to organise a 'One Earth Gathering' alive in our hearts, our small group stood together in a circle somewhere outside Bangor and, hands linked, eyes closed, we asked to be guided to the place where this event could materialise. Minutes passed until one of us spoke.

I think we need to cross the bridge and go on to Anglesey.

No one questioned the suggestion and we travelled across the Menai Bridge to the island. There again, we followed the same procedure, and this time we received the guidance to travel to the island's eastern peninsula. The details are sketchy in my mind, but some time later we were walking up the driveway of an imposing manor house, beating on the door and announcing to the owner that we believed his property to be the venue for the next 'One Earth Gathering'. To our surprise, bewilderment and delight, this new friend instantly agreed. The manor house we had discovered was located on a hillside that looked south to the mountains of Snowdonia on the mainland; it was a breathtaking view. Although we knew that Anglesey was the druids' ancient island stronghold, we had no knowledge of the deeper story that lay folded into the grass, rocks and earth of our new discovery. The One Earth Gathering came and went; it touched us all and we found inspiration. In our different ways, we set about the far harder task of taking this vision to a world that, for the most part, showed only partial interest.

On this hillside I drew a circle and created a garden. I planted myself in the rhythmic mystery of earth and sky and strove to listen well. I did not know that, below me on a shoreline, almost within sight, 4000 Batavian auxiliaries under the command of Gaius Suetonius Paulinius had emerged from the sea in 60 CE and, fully armed on horseback, set about their killing work.

> On the beach stood the adverse array, a serried mass of arms and men, with women flitting between the ranks. In the style of Furies, in robes of deathly black and with dishevelled hair, they brandished their torches; while a circle of druids, lifting their hands to heaven and showering imprecations, struck the troops with such an awe at the extraordinary spectacle that, as though their limbs were paralysed, they exposed their bodies to wounds without an attempt at movement. Then, reassured by their general, and inciting each other never to flinch before a band of females and fanatics, they charged behind the standards, cut down all who met them, and enveloped the enemy in his own flames.[4]

I did not know that the attack faltered when the soldiers almost succumbed to their terror of the druids' magic. I did not know that the assault on Mona was one of the final chapters in collapsing a culture that, contrary to popular belief, was complex, advanced in science and mathematics, skilled in

---

[4] Tacitus, *Annals* XIV, xxix–xxx.

engineering, artistically sophisticated and leading the way in the arcane mystery of the smithy and forge. The same culture from which had emerged laws supporting women's rights, of which many twenty-first-century societies find themselves bereft even now. Mona was the spiritual epicentre of Celtic culture during the same period that a baby was born to a carpenter's wife 2244 miles away to the southeast.

Across what we now know as Western Europe, including modern France, Spain, Belgium, the Netherlands and Germany, Mona was a place wreathed in rumour, dreams and legend. It was a holy isle and revered across the tribes. We know very little of the druids, or who they were, and what we do know is of questionable accuracy. It seems likely that they were not a tribe in the sense that the Iceni or Trinovantes were tribes, but more likely an order of teachers, scholars, priests, healers and leaders who were the arbiters of spiritual knowledge and teaching in Celtic society. They were also politically active, and adamant in their rejection of Rome's authority and influence. As such, they were feared and hated by Rome. If their influence had been less widespread, perhaps they would have escaped the wrath of the legions but everywhere Rome experienced insurrection the tell-tale footprint of the druids' influence was evident. It was, perhaps, inevitable that one day a Roman general would forge the hazardous journey through Ordovician territory and, by breaking Mona, break the people whose inspiration she was.

> Perhaps it is not surprising that the most savage and devastating wars Rome ever fought were against the Jews and the Britons, since Judaism and Druidry had a strong political bias and the passions they aroused were directed against Rome with a fanaticism which could be broken only by a crushing defeat that destroyed the majority of the devotees.[5]

---

[5] Graham Webster, *Boudica: The British Revolt Against Rome AD 60* (1978). Reproduced with kind permission of B. T. Batsford, part of Pavilion Books Company Limited.

When I marked out the circular garden I was responding to intuitions and dreams that were wreathed in mist, like the weathered tracks of an animal long gone; faded into the landscape, visible only to fox or stoat. I could not see clearly, but I glimpsed and felt a parallel world. More than this, I could sense an invitation. Measuring and marking the turf, straightening a stiff and aching back to look out across the straits to Eryri, Land of the Eagles; I was setting my compass for a life to come. Without knowing why, I began carving spirals and all kinds of other images arising from my subconscious. I responded to the myth of elders who had once gathered and taught on this hillside, and I began to remember things I had been taught to dismiss. I discovered the vestiges of an ability to see into the dark and, in the manner of the bumbling amateur I was, I reached into the recesses.

In the late Iron Age, Britain's landscape was not a wilderness of forest, bog and heath. The human population at this time was somewhere between 1.5 and 2.5 million (we are currently 65 million in 2016 and growing), and a pattern of fields, farms, roads and villages was already established. We had long since put aside the nomadic freedom of hunter-gatherers for the settled, backbreaking security of farming. Approximately thirty tribes occupied the available land, and it seems likely that there was great diversity in language, dialects and customs.

However, for all their differences, our indigenous ancestors inhabited the same cosmological worldview and shared beliefs that were probably consistent with many other animistic and shamanic religions. Trade routes were well-established with other tribes in mainland Europe, and it is inevitable that Rome was a topic frequently debated in the dark intimacy of our tribal roundhouses. Exotic goods were trickling into the villages and reports of unimaginable wealth would, as ever, have tempted some to advocate collaboration. A new pantheon of gods and goddesses accompanied the assertive new power, and many would have been incredulous at the stories of a military phenomenon of unimaginable strength. As rumours spread, exciting some to throwing open their doors and others to sharpening swords, the druids' own highly developed, expansive and subterranean network seems to have drawn its own conclusion: *Rome must be resisted at all costs.*

The druids were not limited to Britain, since their order reached out across many parts of the known world and included people from diverse tribes and regions. Alert to Rome's ambitions and to the necessity of being well-informed on many political, military and territorial issues, it seems likely that the druids maintained a regular flow of information to and from Mona. In addition to this, many young men and women desiring to join the order would have travelled long distances from the tribal regions of Britain and beyond. They were travelling to an island that would have held many dreams and fears for them, especially as they contemplated the two decades of training that it involved. As they always have, young men and women – people searching for greater fulfilment, for a life resonant with meaning – were prepared to walk into the unknown.

In the early spring of 2008 I walked up the track that leads through the west yurt village on my way to Embercombe's stone circle. Traversing through the fields, I found a comfy spot and sat on the grass tussocks just outside the stone circle, among the oak trees that had so mysteriously appeared a few years earlier. I allowed my mind to still, gently reviewing insights and understandings that had emerged from my experience of our 'civilised' world. We had lost connection, both with nature and with the animated cosmological perspective that had sustained our culture for hundreds, and perhaps thousands, of years. We had broken our pledge to the Children's Fire, and to each other. We had chosen to elevate the vacuous and the superficial above that which our hearts more wisely knew to be true, and our vision of the future belonged only to those who sold us 'stuff'. It was then, and it is now, clear to me that we have to reclaim this world of ours. Wresting it back from a tired, arthritic ideology that presupposes humanity's destiny to be lording it over everything else; the apex of the pyramid, the evolutionary equivalent of Mozart's last symphony, No. 41. The same set of beliefs and assumptions that are enthusiastically tipping us towards the delusionary madness of self-annihilation. The chief leaned towards me.

'Until the day comes that the people of your islands remember their sacred duty to love and care for the Earth, the Children's Fire will remain extinguished. Until they remember that the thrushes, the rabbits, the trees and all waters also belong to and are loved by creation, there will be no justice. Until ceremonies are held honouring the seasons, and the youth are held by elders worthy of that name, there will be no lasting peace. Until this day comes, we will always be frightened of your people, for you see with dead eyes and your madness may be all it takes to tip the scales.'

She paused, and then, whispering: 'Mend what was broken. Rekindle the Children's Fire.'

Chapter 2
The Land, Our Land

once, there was clay.
before that, burning lava.
now, you are here.

ice once covered everything.
floods drowned the helpless.
yet you live.

we are sons of survivors
daughters of destruction.

our ancestors are rocks
thrusting upwards from some impossible yesterday.
our grandparents are not just adam and eve
but the ripening fruit on the tree
the serpent with eyes aflame
the jealous god and his parting gifts.

inside of us pulsing rainforests
collide with snow cut mountains,
upon whose faces sit ridges of teeth
that belong to the laughing face
of the beloved.

she is laughing at you.

for you chose life while others chose death
you beat a path through the undergrowth while
others
followed suspiciously straight roads.

listen. let me tell you a secret.

your wound
is a womb
from which
new life
will grow.

— *hidden treasure*, by tommy crawford
the right kind of trouble

THERE IS A mound at Embercombe that is satisfyingly shaped
to provide a wonderful lookout post, from which to watch
the sunrises and sunsets, the panorama of woodland, meadows,
hills and the sights and sounds of people going about their lives.
A spiralling footpath describes half of an ascending figure-of-
eight until it arrives at the small, flattened summit. It is located
at the end of the track that leads from our main public entrance;
all that is left of the 1000-metre airstrip that once launched itself
along this spur of hillside. At the point where the light aircraft
would have lifted off above the Teign River valley, marking the
boundary of Dartmoor National Park, the mound now stands
sentinel. Almost four miles to the south, located at the base of
a limestone rock outcrop, there are a number of caves. They are
still not fully explored but over the years the bones of sabre-
toothed tiger, hyena, cave bear, lynx, deer, wolf, auroch, reindeer
and Ice-Age woolly rhinos have been found. The cave penetrates
150 feet into the cliff with a ceiling height of five feet, and was
once home to our own species, as numerous flint implements
and tools bear testimony. With Embercombe so close by, it is
almost certain that our distant relatives foraged and hunted in
this valley, walking the same hill, perhaps drinking from the

same spring, looking out west at the weather coming in over the uplands we now call Dartmoor. This land is old; it has history and story. Buried beneath the pavements and roads upon which we mostly walk, this history sleeps.

It was on the mound one morning that I began to consider more deeply a plan that had coalesced into my conscious mind with the stealth of something known in the body before it is understood in the mind. A long time ago, perhaps shortly before 78 CE when Gnaeus Julius Agricola, the newly appointed Governor of Britain, returned to Mona to finish the job that Suetonius Paulinus had begun some eighteen years earlier, we might have observed the last aspirant druid travelling to Mona. She, or he, would not have been there for long. Perhaps their training was never completed, or perhaps they were smuggled away to Hibernia (Ireland), or north to the fastness of Caledonian territory, to continue their initiatory training. Either way, the spiritual authority of Mona was finished and, with the new Roman fortress of Segontium now crouched on the mainland coast, many hearts must have burst at the grief of such complete and thorough defeat. Eyes half-closed, sat on Embercombe's mound 2000 years later, I could see the howls of grief drift, like vapour among the now-fallen sacred oaks. Desecrated, raped, the viscera of a people's deep dreaming torn from the slit belly of the goddess, and spread for the dying to witness, as breath became wind.

High above the mound, two ravens flew west speaking an archaic language, and inviting my attention.

What if we fell, yet were never defeated? What if the swords laid us down on the soft earth and, even as our bodies decomposed, we slept, but in our dying also dreamed of returning? What if a distant relative was to walk the journey again, travelling from tribal homelands on the mainland to the Isle of Mona, to reclaim what had been lost and to mend our broken circle? As I considered this journey, I knew of some who hold that the spirit of the holy isle has long since departed – the portals of a mysterious past forever closed; the spring waters fouled and no longer flowing. It felt plausible. Visiting Anglesey, not many find the hair rising on the back of their necks and visions crowding more mundane preoccupations into second place. It is very easy to allow our own experiences to become submerged under the opinions of others. I reflected on the impactful events that had drawn me to create a prayer garden, rooted in the spiritual philosophy of indigenous America, on Mona; of my Native American mentors' entreaty to reassert the idea of my land as sacred; of the car accident that had plunged me into an existential crisis, a confrontation with death and the choice of life at precisely the time I marked out the garden on Mona. I reflected upon the arrival of Gerry, who brought me an extraordinary story. Gerry was a former Special Boat Services soldier, and I have never met anyone who looked more 'soldier' than Gerry. His build, his bearing, his classic square-jawed, bullet-headed appearance, the ever-alert eyes, the hurt that hid beneath the toughness and the desolate loneliness of a man separated from comrades whose companionship had served his need for meaning. Retired from service, he had been earning a living training ETA, the Basque nationalist separatist organisation, sharing the skills he had honed in countless conflict zones around the world. Gerry was tormented with a recurring dream. He had been experiencing this dream for many years, sometimes every night for days on end. In the dream, he was a Roman legionnaire. During a skirmish somewhere in the mountains of Snowdonia, Ordovician tribal territory, he had been separated from his contubernia, or squadron. Exhausted and frightened, yet employing all the skills and discipline instilled in him over many campaigns, he was desperately trying to reach the security of his legion. Taking risks, doubling back on his tracks, trying to anticipate his enemy, he knew that the tribal trackers were closing in on him. The dream would extend itself along the gaunt, rock-strewn valleys separating the mountains, through swampy woodland and along ancient track ways. His breath, coming in great heaving sobs, stifling thoughts of the farm he had always hoped to own, shocked at the imminence of death, he spun to the sound of a stick snapping. No mercy in the eyes of his foes, only the vast hatred of everything he stood for. Blade after blade hacking, cleaving, smashing and puncturing his tired, broken and despairing body; then, darkness and a life spilling into the moss and heather of a land he neither knew nor understood.

Far away from home. This dream, again and again, always the same, never different. Gerry had no theories with which to probe this recurrent nightmare. He knew that he had lived this life. And so he had found his way back to Mona, at a different time and in a different life, in his own way, seeking redemption, forgiveness and peace. He came to Mona and an executive leadership centre, where the gardener was also yielding to a related dream of the same time – perhaps one of those who wielded the swords that bled his life away. Though Gerry had committed many acts of violence and not always with the excuse of fighting for a good cause, I knew him to be kind and generous. He is dead now, again and, perhaps somewhere in time and space, the same soul continues its journey towards wholeness and love.

And then, another traveller arrived at the same place, washed up on the shores of Mona, with another good story to tell. Like many carriers of stories, he was not aware that he was walking his story towards some kind of assignation. Branton was tall, with long flaxen hair and the mien of one who assumed leadership. At some point he revealed to me that he was directly related to General George Armstrong Custer, who led the US 7th Cavalry Regiment to its destruction at the Battle of Little Bighorn in 1876, against a confederation of Cheyenne and Sioux. The tribes had left their reservations in outraged response to the repeated incursions of white settlers into the Black Hills, land sacred to the Great Sioux Nation. So here we were, a small gathering. A gardener beset with dreams and intuitions that tugged him back to a different time, while also offering a vision of living a contemporary life in a different way. A twentieth-century gardener, scribing a living prayer into the soil of Mona, once the spiritual heartland of his people, mentored by Native Americans to rediscover his incipient indigeny alongside a Custer lookalike and relative of the same notorious Indian killer. A Special Forces soldier, snared in dreams that, in spite of his greatest efforts, held his face to a hot fire, scorched his scepticism and practised courage, and somehow parachuted him into the very place his ancient Roman memory most feared.

I have no doubt that the day I took up residence on Anglesey, I accepted the invitation to an initiatory journey that would enable me to advocate on behalf of our Earth with some fluency and power.

Anglesey, the Isle of Mona, is still dreaming the old dream and her dreaming is powerful. She may never be what she once was, and she may not overwhelm the casual observer with her appearance, but then much that once bloomed has endured the same casual disrespect and suffered the ignorance that judges, assesses and dismisses. I have no sense of Mona's future destiny because, like the hag that she is, she keeps her secrets hidden. I only know that I am grateful for the numinous and sometimes excruciating experiences that helped me see that which had been invisible, and that so stridently demanded my attention.

All visions, at some point in time, have to take account of practical realities. In contemplating my journey from Embercombe to Mona, there were a number of realities that I had to negotiate. Living in Devon, I inhabit ancient Dumnonii tribal land, and a brief glance at a road map suggested that if I walked from Embercombe to Mona in 2009, I would either have to follow close by the M5 motorway and then negotiate the industrial complex of Avonmouth before circumnavigating Bristol, or cross the Bristol Channel to Newport or some other South Wales coastal town. With all the competing demands of sitting on Embercombe's management team, facilitating programmes and the treadmill of emails, phone calls and meetings, which in significant part fed our cash-flow, I could only manage to take one month to complete my journey. Since much of the magic of this journey was walking into the unknown, I did not want to undertake trips to Devon's north coast having pre-arranged passage across the Bristol Channel. Equally, I did not fancy arriving on some north Devon clifftop having traversed the Exmoor hills, and face the possibility of days spent searching for an obliging fisherman to ferry me across it. In addition to this, I was not at all sure that I could walk the distance to Mona in the time I had available. This was largely due to six considerations: my work commitments; the imaginal; the weather; navigation; my food; and daylight versus darkness.

I wanted to undertake my journey in January. This was the least frenetic month for my work, and a time when I could disappear with least inconvenience to myself and to others. It is also the deep wintertime of our land, the weeks that pre-empt the Celtic festival of Imbolc, the dreaming that nourishes the first stirring of the awakening year. The journey I envisaged was a walk into the death-ground of our land – a walk that united the past, the present and the future. I wanted to hunker down into the raw wound of an ancient history, and remember. There is a magic in all the seasons and, if I was pushed to name a favourite, I would choose the springtime, close to when I was born; but when it comes to dreaming, remembering, seeing into the darkness of old songs and stories, I choose the deep winter. Intoxicating and evocative as this was, the harsh truth of the weather often served in January was never far from my mind. However, the reason why I have many stories to tell is no doubt partly due to my enduring habit of shoving inconvenient information to the periphery of my mind and vaguely hoping that, when the time comes, I will find the means to eventually prevail.

I had decided to navigate without a compass or map. During the months and weeks before, it was tempting to sneak a glance or two at the ordnance survey maps scattering my bookshelf, but I decided not to. I wanted to walk into the unknown, and find my way using the sun and the stars. Of course, I also possessed a general knowledge of Britain's geography, and I had driven across Wales on several occasions, but I chose to consider this information in the same way that travellers would always have benefited from the advice and directions of others who had made the journey before. Polaris is the current pole star. In 3000 BCE, Thuban in the constellation of Draco was the pole star and in 3000 CE, Gamma Cephei will take over from Polaris. The pole star is the only star that appears not to move in the night sky, and due to its location above the North Pole, it provides the traveller with a reliable fixed point from which to make calculations. In my case, being able to establish north using Polaris, and knowing that Mona was approximately north of Embercombe, would allow me to set my course each night, before I slept. Although our elementary education will have taught us that the sun rises in the east and sets in the west, many of us who live with a view of the surrounding countryside will have noticed that there is a big difference between where the sun both rises and sets between midwinter and midsummer; ninety degrees of difference, in fact.

In England, the midwinter sun rises in the southeast and sets in the southwest. Knowing this, I could expect the sun to be angled towards the rear of my right shoulder in the morning, and the rear of my left shoulder in the afternoon, if I was walking in a northerly direction. Armed with this crudely adequate information, I felt confident that, between Polaris and the sun, I could navigate sufficiently well to meet my needs, providing, of course, that I could see either one or both of my celestial guides. That proviso weighed on my mind, somewhat. The fifth consideration was that I wanted to support the deeper intention of my journey by preparing and carrying food that, for the most part, I had grown or foraged. I had no idea how long the walk would take me. The weather, navigational miscalculations, mishaps, exhaustion and poor choices that could result in extra hours or days of walking all made it difficult to estimate my likely progress. After reflecting on these thoughts, and with some disappointment, I came to the conclusion that I needed to start from somewhere north of Bristol. It was not difficult to find the alternative. It came to me with a jolt, a kind of sudden calm and peaceful resolution. I was born in Great Malvern in Worcestershire, with the Malvern Hills close by. With the eight-mile ridge running on a north-south axis, you can look out from the hilltops towards Herefordshire and beyond to Wales. Mona is 109 miles to the northwest, as the crow flies. It is a lot more if, without the benefit of an aerial view, burdened with a rucksack, in January, and no longer endowed with full, youthful vigour, the crow walks. I decided that walking from the place of my birth to Mona was at least as symbolically significant as the original plan, and perhaps even more so. With some relief at being able to shed the nightmarish vision of bivouacking on the fringes of the M5 motorway, hiding from the police and forced into ignominious defeat, I settled on beginning my journey from the Iron-Age hillfort known as the British Camp.

It is tempting to plan our journeys into submission, to take all the uncertainty and risk that sends us sleepless into the night with the thrilling fear of the unknown, and crush it to death with common sense and sensible precaution. I do not suffer from this affliction. Instead – and, I suspect, partly as a way of managing anxiety – I bury myself in those aspects of the adventure that appeal to my imagination, or allow me to indulge my many idiosyncrasies. An avoidance strategy, perhaps, which skirts the challenge of appraising complexity, for fear that the outcome might imply action that thwarts the decisions I have already unconsciously made. Prior to any undertaking that excites me, I have frequently noticed my tendency towards dreamy, introspective activity that persists in the form of detailed, almost obsessive preparation of something that, in retrospect, is of only marginal value. This kind of activity is all the more satisfying if it involves sights, sounds, smells and sensations that are pleasurable to my senses. Few things are more deeply relaxing to me than tasks undertaken outdoors, with no external imposed pressures regarding outcome or time, well-made tools of quality and a visible, tangible, physically significant result that is only obtainable through the sustained application of mindless, repetitive work. Seated on a stool, cleaning a vast pile of used bricks still encrusted with old mortar, I am free to leap aback the joyful curve of my imagination and take flight. Comforted all the while by the sound of the lump hammer on the cold chisel, the chisel on the mortar, the brick as it is released and arcs to the pile on my right – one pile forever and imperceptibly growing smaller, the other lazily growing towards its brief destiny as a miniature Mount Kilimanjaro. I will often prefer the infinitely longer process of employing a hand tool to the much swifter and more efficient power tool. It is not just dogged conservatism, but the physical pleasure I experience in hefting a favourite tool that has accustomed itself to my hands. The aesthetic and sensuous joy in the interplay between a beautiful handcrafted tool, earth, wood, muscle and breath. My preparation was almost exclusively orientated towards deepening into the dream of my journey, and rather less to the practical consideration of my clothing and equipment. Later on, I had cause to regret this.

The outer physical journey was a mirror of the inner dream journey. One without the other made no sense to me. I would walk the invisible path of my dreaming consciously, while awake, plaiting the two trails, like the threads of a rope. Since I can remember, I have walked in a landscape that is inhabited by a visceral invisible. I feel and sense things long before I understand them, and this was cause for a lot of doubt and confusion when I was younger. Appearances would belie that of which my intuition, feelings and senses informed me; atmospheres, the shadow of past trauma, the unspoken, the madness of our 'values-less', consumption-based society masquerading as progress. It is as if someone gradually tuned the focusing mechanism, and the picture became clear. So, my journey preparation more closely resembled an unplanned emergent ceremony than the organised precision of the practised rambler. Being this way, it provided me with a profoundly rich few months – a time when I could slowly submerge into the dream pathway. I walked into the myth in the same way that I will peel back the duvet tonight, and sigh with pleasure as the bed reaches out to welcome me home.

I began with acorns. I was brought up to believe that acorns are inedible for humans. Even as a child, I thought this to be very unfortunate, inconvenient and wasteful, since with some variation there is often a harvest of these conveniently sized nuts, and gathering them is fun and rewarding. I have always loved setting off with a basket or bag and foraging, then returning home and sorting, before processing and eventually using my precious treasure to some good end. In fact, acorns *are* edible, providing that you use one of several methods to leach out the tannins that our stomachs cannot tolerate. Squirrels and jays also gather and stash acorns during the autumn, and it may be that their habit of burying them in the earth allows a natural leaching process to occur before consumption later in the year. Wherever oak trees grow, acorns have provided food for people at a time of year when other sources of nutrition are in short supply. Particularly valuable in the Palaeolithic era must have been the carbohydrates that the acorn's starch provided. With all the enthusiasm of the recent convert, I prowled our woodland and hedges, returning home with baskets overflowing. Briefly simmering the nuts in boiling water, I shelled the acorns and then began leaching the tannins by repeatedly dunking the nuts in hot water, waiting for them to turn brown and then pouring off the water before starting again. In retrospect, I think that if I had chopped them up first, I might have greatly accelerated the process. However, not only was efficiency not a priority, I was enjoying myself. The acorns were lightly toasted and ground, filling a large box that was then stashed on a shelf, as I turned my attention to drying venison strips and apple rings, and grinding some wheat grain that I had grown some years before.

Embercombe is located on an upland area, much of which is now densely forested. Providing cover for a large population of menalistic (black) fallow deer, 3500 acres of coniferous plantations swathe the hills. Until recently, it was thought that the

Normans introduced the deer to Britain; however, archaeological exploration at Fishbourne Roman Palace in Sussex shows that fallow deer were introduced into southern Britain some time in the first century CE, and since that time they have flourished. Conversations about the ethics of killing animals and eating meat have provided our community with endless opportunities for practising peaceful communication between peoples or groups that hold strong and radically differing beliefs and opinions. The issue was resolved for me during a ceremony with my Native American mentors. When the next deer arrived and was being skinned by a supervised group of visiting teenagers, I bought one of the haunches and began preparing venison jerky, drying strips of meat on a rack above my wood stove.

Apples were harvested from a small tree that I had planted seven years previously and had positioned just outside the living room window. These, I cut into rings and also dried. The shelf holding the jars, bags and pots of my journey food was steadily filling and, as the days shortened, the nights grew longer. I turned my attention to a bin filled with ears of wheat. In the early years of Embercombe's emergence, I fulfilled a long-held dream and grew a field of wheat. It was an older, long-stemmed variety and it grew well on our rich clay loam. The unsustainable industrial farming practices of commodity wheat production, and the burgeoning incidence of gluten intolerance, has cast a shadow over wheat, but I remain a lover of this wild grass relative as others have before me, even for 7000 years. With wheat grain taking some 110 to 130 days between sowing and harvesting, and mindful of our fitful weather, I decided to sow winter wheat so that it would have the best chance to ripen before wind and rain threatened the harvest. If there was ever a lesson in the virtues of wild food foraging versus the labour of agriculture, this was it. The soil was ploughed and then later harrowed twice. Carefully dividing the circle of land for cultivation into four quarters, and the seed into four separate pots, together with some friends I hand-sowed the seed. All through the year I would gaze in wonderment at the green waves that rippled and danced as the wheat grew tall. Then, the lengthening summer and green gave way to gold, even eventually to silver. Now the field's song changes, and sighs give way to rustling shivers of taut expectancy. With the soil possibly too rich, and the ears of corn plump and heavy on long stems, my crop yielded to a late summer gale and 'lodged'; large areas were laid to the earth and far more difficult to harvest. We laboured under a very hot sun, scything and sheaving all we could. By the end of the weekend my now mostly erstwhile friends were broken in spirit and body. Using a tiny grinder, we made a small mound of flour and baked a few bread rolls. They were delicious and ravenously devoured, as we lay in the coarse August grass, silent, staring into the middle distance, awed and intimidated at our ancestor's true grit. Most of this group of volunteers never returned to Embercombe, and I am not convinced that this was because they were inspired to dedicate their talents towards the kind of 'sustainable world' that they had just experienced. After everyone had gone, I continued the journey of rendering my labours fruitful. It was long and hard. The wheat was eventually brought in to the only indoor dry space I had, and filled the barn approximately twenty by thirty metres and one metre deep. Threshing with flails was one of the hardest, most exhausting things I have ever done, and it took a very long time. The arrival of the rats finished me off. One afternoon, wearily trudging up the hill and bracing myself for another few hours of backbreaking work, I flung open the sliding doors of the barn and prompted a stampede of rats, who broke cover from the wheat and raced past me – lots and lots and lots of rats, rat droppings everywhere. Further efforts were made to salvage the harvest, but by this time defeat was inevitable and simply awaiting my surrender. It was with mixed feelings when, a few years later, I checked the very last remaining bin of wheat ears to see if they were still in good enough condition for my journey to Mona. In some ways, it felt like the last remaining act I could envisage that might in some way redeem my foray into agriculture. From this bin I made more flour than the mountain of wheat I had grown and processed before. Most of the former had found its way to the hens. It was with quiet satisfaction and some humility that I added two bags of home-grown wheat flour to the shelf, and then stood back to admire the victuals that would sustain me over the fast-approaching January of 2009.

Ever since the Second World War, when German submarines were wreaking havoc with the British merchant fleet that was bringing in all kinds of essential goods, including fruit and vegetables, rosehips have been celebrated for their very high vitamin C content. On 29 September 1941, a national week for the collection of rosehips was organised by the British Government to gather the abundant and valuable harvest.[6] Across the country, rosehips were gathered by foraging enthusiasts and then gifted to selected firms, who processed them into syrup sold at affordable prices. It seemed to me that syrup that was potent with vitamin C and very sweet might be a welcome and comforting addition to dried venison, wheat flour, apple rings and acorns. Like the droplets from a flung paintbrush, the red-orange hips were now clustering the hedgerows, and I spent a very happy afternoon filling several bags. Like acorn gathering, I experienced the same peaceful, even joyful sense of ancient memory. The rosehips were processed according to the wartime recipe included in the Ministry of Food's leaflet 'Hedgerow Harvest', and with it, my food preparations were complete. I turned my attention to my kit. There is something profoundly aesthetically displeasing to me about most outdoor clothing. It looks and feels slick. Nonetheless, there was a vague disquiet periodically asserting itself in my mind and, although I love the rigour of cold and some hardship, I also love comfort. An inhabitant of Sparta and Sybaris by turn, I relished the thought of profound physical discomfort rewarded by its opposite. My

---

[6] The Old Foodie, Wednesday, 28 May 2014. www.theoldfoodie.com/2014/05/the-rose-hip-collection-campaign-ww-ii.html.

old down sleeping bag had abandoned its vocation and now felt like two thin, limp sheets of nothing. It was extremely light and filled a tiny stuff bag, but it was inadequate. I resolved to purchase a bag with a synthetic filler, since the disadvantage of extra weight seemed worth the advantage of its capacity to provide warmth, even if wet. To a greater or lesser extent, wet felt inevitable; however, the warmer the bag, the heavier it gets, and I was already becoming a little nervous of just how much weight I might find myself carrying. I chose a bag that said it would keep me warm to temperatures of −12°C. A nonchalant, amenable and, in hindsight, entirely inadequate conversation with a sales assistant at a specialist outdoor activity store led me to accept his advice. It was, he affirmed, extremely unlikely that the weather in Wales would plunge below −6°C. Primarily still fixated about the bag's weight, I chose to accept this advice and moved on to the next items on my list: boots, a waterproof jacket and a water purifier. The water purifier was a delight; a tiny little pump marketed with Ray Mears' endorsement and sufficient for my needs, this single item proved to be indispensable. Walking across Wales in January, I never imagined that access to water would be problematic.

As December advanced and work slowed at Embercombe, the dawning truth of this journey sank deeper. I was both excited and nervous. With the guidance of friends still living in North Wales, I drove north and crossed on to Anglesey, searching for a place where I could end my journey. A small ring of iron, dated to the early years of the first century CE, had come into my possession. It had been authenticated as part of a chariot harness and discovered in Norfolk – Iceni tribal territory. In the late Iron Age, the tribes in Britain were famous for their horsemanship and still used chariots in battle. It seemed more than possible that the chariot to which this ring of iron once belonged could have been actively used within the same period that the Iceni, led by Boudica, made its final and fateful challenge to Roman authority, the challenge that led to its downfall and sealed the fate of Mona. I intended to carry this remnant of tribal freedom from my home in Dumnonii territory (Devon and Cornwall), via the British Camp, skirting Silures territory as I travelled west, and then up through Ordovician land until I reached Mona. I needed a place where I could complete my ceremonial walk, a place that might once have been visited and considered sacred to the ancestors by the druids. Bryn Celli Ddu (the Mound in the Dark Grove) is a passage tomb, and one of the most intriguing of its kind. It was worth investigating. Archaeological excavations suggest that some kind of ceremonial site had been constructed here approximately 4000 years ago, in the Mesolithic period. A thousand years later it was reconstructed as a henge with a stone pit, at the base of which was placed a single human ear-bone. Here was a place of archaic silence, a place to listen. Another thousand years later the site was again developed, this time as a passage tomb and then, after repeated use, large stones were placed across the entrance, sealing the passage. In the centre of the chamber there is a two-metre-high, single vertical rounded stone and in a location that would once have been inside the tomb there is another stone with strange serpentine shapes scrolled into both sides. Although the site has been plundered, dismantled, reconstructed and reinstated, somehow it still retains some mystery. I resolved to make Bryn Celli Ddu my final destination – the place to which I would carry the Iceni chariot ring and whisper the words that might signal a remembering of a time when we knew our land was sacred, and her people free. The ring touching the stone would sound a note within the dreaming earth; the despair of a broken people would rally to the knowledge that a path had been found through the brambled defences of something holy, defiled and left to lurch, screaming into the grey netherworld of old memory.

***

The land around Embercombe is formed by a fifteen-mile line of hills, which blocks the way deeper into the southwest. This upland area was moorland not so long ago, and all along its flanks are valleys and hills that, like all borderlands, have seen the feverish activity of humans enacting their small and large dramas for many centuries. Early Neolithic settlements 4000 years old are in evidence, along with numerous Bronze-Age tumuli and an Iron-Age fortress. Ancient trackways, including one of Roman origin, thread across the hills and, while it hosts several thousand acres of regimented forestry plantation, it is nevertheless a beautiful and ecologically important area. Rising to a height of 250 metres, these hills would have provided wary defenders with many vantage points from which to observe the intentions of unwelcome others. Wedged into the southwest edge of the forest, Embercombe is a small fifty-acre valley with a rise of about sixty metres from its lowest to highest point. The land around is rucked into steep-sided curving valleys, sunken lanes with extravagant twists, high hedges and expensive property. In the curious way of these things, the value of these hills has been perceived very differently by succeeding generations.

I was reclined on a sofa slurping tea, my tongue searching out the last remaining crumbs of a mince pie. Relaxed and confident, as it is easy to be when in such circumstances, I was staring at my rucksack. It was finally packed and was perched on the floor with a kind of plump self-important expectancy. I accepted a top-up to my outstretched mug and briefly struggled with an overwhelming desire to doze off again. Another festive-season lunch was settling in my gut, and the imminent journey felt very remote.

'Perhaps I should try it on?', spoken more to myself than to anyone else. The rucksack maintained its nonchalant disinterest and continued to squat fatly on the living room floor. Outside, the temperature was dropping, as chilled Arctic air insinuated itself among the silent valleys. Like many of Embercombe's sofas, the one I was sitting in was a lot easier to get into than out of. I jerked and shuffled my way to a place from which I could lurch forwards and upwards. It all felt very demanding and inconvenient. There is a short sequence in the movie *Wild*, in which Reese Witherspoon, taking the part of Cheryl

Strayed, attempts to leverage her rucksack on to her back as she undergoes final preparations for her US Pacific Crest Trail journey. The rucksack is massive, passive and unco-operative. It was the same with mine; in my already self-inflicted weakened state I was no match for the obduracy I encountered. It really did feel shockingly heavy.

Doing my best not to submit to a sudden onrush of hopelessness, I rallied and became more focused in my efforts. Finally, and now shocked into the truth of my situation, I managed to hoist my pack into position and stood, swaying, looking out from the house to the frosty disdain of the great outdoors. Tottering through the hall, and conscious of remaining bolt upright in case my centre of gravity precipitated a sudden uncontrollable descent, I opened the front door with the intention of doing a short test walk. The mildly hilly and idyllic eccentricities of my surroundings almost immediately assumed a malefic tone. Leaning forwards slightly, so that the weight of my pack pitched me forward, I wobbled ahead and began to ascend the short, steep lane that leaps up to the ridge above our land. I began, and then I stopped. The vague discomfiture of a few minutes ago gave way to rising despair. 'Shit; twenty metres on a small hill and I'm fuc...' The hill came and went, and I reached Embercombe's main public entrance after walking about one kilometre. I was bewildered and fighting a sense of panic. During this short distance, my body had remembered something that I had long since forgotten. I had felt a weakness in my hips that I remembered from much, much earlier days, only now it felt more vulnerable. Coming back through our fields and along the track leading past the circular garden, I was silent, preoccupied with assimilating the information that I had received. I would have to make some changes; I would have to lose some of the weight I was carrying.

The next day saw me undertaking the same short journey, but now the atmosphere had changed and a dispassionate, rational mind had taken charge. Festive indulgence was behind me, and I was fully concentrated on ensuring that I was making decisions that fully accounted for the horrible reckoning of the previous day. Half of my food supplies were jettisoned, extra clothing was cast aside, various desirable but unnecessary utensils disappeared and some objects that had only aesthetic or sentimental value followed them. It made a big difference. Even so, I could not dispel the gnawing doubt that the first experiment had introduced to me. I knew that, whatever else this journey might be, it was going to be very challenging – both physically and emotionally. I needed to accept, and yet not capitulate to, the fact that being just three months short of sixty years of age, I no longer had the stamina, strength and resilience of the younger man I still secretly thought myself to be. Things had changed.

**

Friday, 2 January 2009, and flames leap to the billowing darkness. The low murmur of voices as essential information is shared. Wood smoke, the fleeting glimpse of the waxing crescent moon, soft drumming and a voice, thin like the between-world wraiths: 'Hey... Ahey... aawhey... aaa...'

The stones glow and pulse in the dragon's lair deep inside the fire. A ring of friends sit hunched, faces livid with gold, amber and pulsing shards of red. All eyes are with the fire.

'Joey...' My voice jarring against the deep contemplative silence; the form that has been shifting and gliding between shadows and flames that snarl defiance at the encircling dark becomes human and steps towards me; this old-soul friend, who touches me so deeply, my friend Joey Bear. There are people whose depth you sense as a palpable force of energy, a spirit almost discernible even without the body, a power of presence that, quite irrationally, moves the tears from their hiding place. Such a man is Joey. People say that Joey is big – and he is, to a degree – but bigness, with Joey, is more a description of his heart and soul than his physical presence. The immense courage of someone who chooses to grasp the charcoal and, with deft swiftness, curve the lines of his own story upon a slate that might once have never been more than grey and utterly predictable. After an unconvincing start, and against all the odds, Joey had chosen life.

We stand together, two men from different sides of town, grown deeply fond of each other, recognition between us that has always risen above words and found itself in our shared love of life and the wandering misted pathway. 'Joey... is everything ready?'

For years now, there has been a furore burning within many Native American circles at the misappropriation of their sacred ceremonies. Having endured the invasion and theft of their homelands, the physical, psychological, cultural and spiritual devastation of their people and way of life – having experienced all of this, the theft and perversion of their sacred ceremonies is a knife that cuts deep. I think back to the early '80s when, with a small group of male friends, we built our first Inipi, or sweat lodge. We had read Black Elk's 'The Sacred Pipe'[7] and our imaginations were fired. For several years, and in our own inimitable manner, the Mountain Group launched itself into the high mountains of Snowdonia, sought visions and received them aplenty. Our gardens, psilocybin mushrooms, the mountains and Black Elk's words sank deep into the nascent dreams of belonging and becoming. We took his words to be an invitation, and it never occurred to us that we might be stealing something that was not ours. During this period, one of our group, Osman, purchased a First Nation's pipe bowl at a market stall in London. Pasted on the flattened sole of the pipe bowl was a small note stating that it was found in Blackfoot tribal territory. It was not made of Catlinite, the familiar red stone of the Pipestone National Monument, but rather of a very fine green stone with which we were unfamiliar. With great care and precision,

---

[7] Black Elk, *The Sacred Pipe: Black Elk's Account of the Seven Rites of the Oglala Sioux* (as told to Joseph Epes Brown), University of Oklahoma Press, 1971.

Osman fashioned a wooden pipe stem and this pipe became the Mountain Group's most treasured sacred prayer object. Thirty-four years later, wrapped in red cloth and inside a case, it awaited destiny's calling. In the early winter of 2013, as I sat in reverie watching the birds break their nighttime fast, it came to me that this pipe should be given back to the Blackfeet Nation. On a 'medicine' journey of its own design, it had somehow found its way across the North American continent and the Atlantic Ocean to Mona, and a small group of young men who were seeking direct spiritual experience. The Mountain Group has not met for many years, and each of us has long since set our own trails, but none of us has forgotten. The smoke that drifted from the pipe bowl wreathed prayers that, even now, play upon the winds and seek to come full-circle. The green stone pipe travelled to a sundance ceremony near Rapid Springs, South Dakota in 2015. At the conclusion of the dance, and beneath the outstretched arms of the cottonwood tree, to which 80 dancers had offered their prayers, the pipe was handed to the Oglala elder Loretta 'Afraid-of-Bear' Cook for safekeeping. She felt into its calling and sent word to Blackfeet relatives; another small step towards healing. Yet, did we misappropriate the Lakota's sacred ceremonies? I am sure that some will say that we did, but I know that a theft undertaken unknowingly and in good faith is less a theft, and more a reflection of cultural nescience. The green stone medicine pipe of the Blackfeet was smoked in a prayerful, if also uninformed, manner. It has been directly instrumental in guiding me to a place where, together with others, I can at least *begin* the long homeward journey towards reclaiming what was once stolen from Britain: the ceremonies of our own tribal indigenous people, the remembering of our broken circle. From the base of the forgotten tree, green shoots sprout and bud, the waters of the dried well flow again, the clouds part and rays of sunlight wash across the land; we can be a people again. This is what was so uplifting in the response my two new Native American friends gave me when they heard the story of the Mountain Group; the story of the pipe. Loretta

'Afraid-of-Bear' Cook of the Lakota and Karonhiénhawe of the Mohawk knew that *spirit* was finding a way through to us, and that all peoples of this saddened world could one day know that they, too, are indigenous – indigenous to the Earth. This most beautiful, magical medicine pipe of the Blackfeet nation undertook a journey to us. It could feel the pulse in our dreaming and it made its way, unerringly. Our dreaming also called the pipe and, between the two powers of the calling and the listening, we were made a sacred gift. Thank goddess that, at some level, we understood. When the pipe stem was made, and one day the stem and the bowl came together, we joined the twin powers of creation. With smoke, prayers could be made. Lit with the glowing ember of a twig drawn from the Inipi fire, the small sun in the bowl of the pipe came alive again on Mona, and unseen powers began to move once more. Indigenous – this is the real meaning of the word; to be indigenous is to possess the soul-knowing of belonging to some small corner of this Earth, to be rooted in the deep flowing and knowing of place and time. When we rediscover our indigeny, the words of apology that twist our features into the dangerous humiliation of the slave collapse and dry, before they have breath to sound their desperate, lonely savagery.

The sauna of Scandinavia was – and for some, at least, still is – a healing ceremony. I asked Maria, a Finnish friend, about this and she wrote back:

> Hi Mac
> Jonathan forwarded me your email regarding the sauna. The word is *löyly* and means spirit or soul. In old Finnish you talked about a man's *löyly* when you meant soul. But it is also the sauna spirit that has a healing power and nurturing and relaxing effect. Among the stones in the sauna you have one stone with holes in it. This stone begins to sing/make a sound when you throw water on [it]. That's the spirit talking.
>
> So Löyly is healing spirit.

The sauna was also the place where you gave birth. It was a warm, clean and spiritual place. My Mum was born in a sauna.

Much love

Maria

Perhaps the ubiquitous sweat houses of Ireland also have their origins in ceremonies long since lost – made invisible by the same planned obfuscation that turned 'cure stones' into 'curse stones' and, perhaps, long ago we did, indeed, have a ceremony very closely similar to the Native American Inipi. I found the following short article on Birmingham City Council's website. It explores the evidence of an archaeological site excavated in 1980/1 at Cob Lane, Bourneville:

The Burnt Mound Mystery – Kitchen or Sauna[8]

Burnt mounds are usually interpreted as the debris from when ancient people made water boil to cook food by dropping heated stones into it. Although experiments have shown that this could have been the case, we would expect to find animal bones and other debris from food preparation and cooking.

Another interpretation is that they are the debris from steam or sauna-type bathing. In North American Indian sweat lodges, steam is produced for bathing by pouring water over heated stones inside a tent or hut. Reconstructions based on the excavated evidence from the Cob Lane site and the structures used by North American Indians have shown that burnt mounds could well have been saunas.

Reconstruction

The reconstruction consists of a hearth on which the stones are heated and a tent on a framework of bent-over branches. The heated stones are placed in a hollow inside the tent and

---

8 www.birmingham.gov.uk/info/50064/birminghams_archaeology/ 972/birmingham_3000_years_ago/1.

water ladled on to them from a clay-lined pit, to produce steam.

This reconstruction replicates all the features found in the Cob Lane excavation: the shattered stones and charcoal which is the debris from the hearth, the holes resulting from the pointed branches used to make the tent, the burnt hollow which is where the hot stones are placed, and the clay-lined pit next to the former stream line.

When Joey opened the door of the ceremonial lodge and I came out into the new day, I was ready for my journey. The circle of friends had mostly departed, the fire was burning low and grey clouds were scudding in from the southeast. Final preparations and farewells were completed, and my gear was loaded into Joey's car; it was time to leave.

We joined the A38 and then headed north on the M5. It all felt very unreal. I was reclining in the passenger seat of Joey's car; the seat was soft and I felt almost infantilised by the way it seemed to wrap itself around me. I was grateful for the fact that this journey would take a few hours and settled myself deeper into the dreamy warm fug of acceptance. We arrived at the Malvern Hills in the early afternoon, but it could as well have been the first few minutes of pre-dawn when, in the frozen numbness of midwinter, all life has retracted and turned towards the dark.

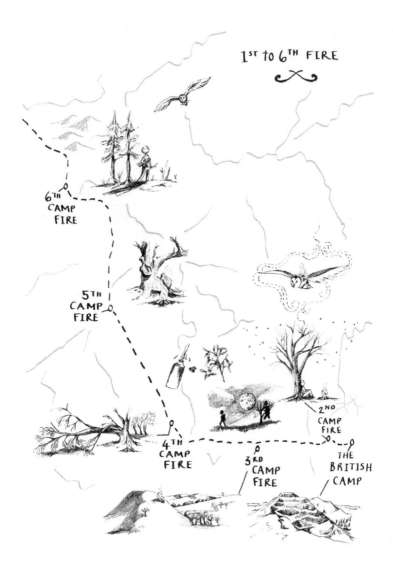

1ST to 6TH FIRE

6TH CAMP FIRE

5TH CAMP FIRE

4TH CAMP FIRE

3RD CAMP FIRE

2ND CAMP FIRE

THE BRITISH CAMP

Map 2

Chapter 3
The Journey, Our Journey

The Winter of 2008/9 brought a mixed bag but overall was cooler than average with some notably cold spells. December started on the cold side before becoming milder after mid-month but between Christmas and New Year the cold returned with a vengeance with a biting easterly wind.

The cold continued into January too before gradually petering out during the second week with the remainder of the month twoing and froing between cooler and milder spells of weather. The cold start meant that it was the coldest January since 2005 in England and Wales.

February started with more cold weather and some significant falls of snow, but the cold slowly eased through the month to leave temperatures close to average overall. The winter as a whole was colder than average though and turned out to be the coldest winter since 1995/96.[9]

---

[9] Netweather, independent weather forecaster in the UK – winter 2008/9. www.netweather.tv/weather-forecasts/uk/winter/winter-history.

Day 1: Friday, 2 January

THE CAR DOOR slammed shut; it seemed very final. Britain was held in a frigid embrace of ice and snow; −4°C and going down. Above us reared the ancient folded earthworks of the British Camp, an Iron-Age fortification located towards the southern end of the Malverns, a single spine of hills bordering two counties in the West Midlands. I jerked my rucksack into position and tightened the waist strap, making a conscious effort to ignore its still profound and discouraging weight. Together with Joey, I made a cautious, winding and precarious ascent towards the hilltop. I wanted to stand on the highest ridge and gaze out west, towards the horizon of my journey. I wanted to see the winter sun go before me, and I wanted to give time to this precious, intimidating moment of beginning. We did not talk, both concentrating on the treacherous film of frost that sparkled and crunched beneath the slow rhythm of our steps. All manner of thoughts and emotions jostled for my attention. Self-doubt flooded every space left unguarded, and I felt the first intimations of impending loneliness. Heads down, we made our way up a shoulder of the hill that was free of other walkers, and I glanced up briefly to gauge the route. Just ahead of me, wrapped in cellophane and incongruous on the frozen hillside, was a bunch of flowers – the price curiously prominent on the wrapping. Somehow, they felt significant, and not only for the lost life that their presence seemed to suggest – not only the mourning of a woman or man, still hurting and seeking a quiet wild place to remember a loved one who was once warm, alive and present, but the mourning of something else that was absent on the flanks of this hill of memories. Standing on top of the British Camp, feet apart and braced against a bitingly cold northeasterly wind, I watched the sun send out great horizontal threads of soft, golden light across a landscape already preparing for the long darkness. A great warrior ancestor of ours, Caratacus, was said to have fought his final battle with the Roman legions here.[10] For more than a decade, he terrorised and humiliated the Roman governor Publius Ostorius Scapula, out-manoeuvring all efforts to defeat his loose coalition of Silures and other free tribespeople gathering to his banner in Britain's western regions. Although the weight of opinion suggests a different site for this last courageous stand, the old hillfort of the Malverns was, in all likelihood, familiar to Caratacus, and may well have been a refuge where he and his guerrilla forces were welcomed and given freshly baked oat bannocks to eat in the warm fug of a friend's roundhouse. It is difficult, perhaps, to comprehend the meaning of this word, 'free', existing as so many of us do without the dread of our doors being stove in, of soldiers burning our homes and washing their madness in our blood. Standing on the ramparts of the British Camp and looking west towards the ancient lands of the Silures and Ordovicci, I could sense the turbulent ocean of emotion surging in the hearts of the long-dead women and men of 50 CE, crowded together, listening to the stories, seeking news of loved ones and drawing strength from a warrior whose name and reputation was already known and feared 1300 miles away, in Rome itself.

Abruptly, I felt the urgency of penetrating cold and diminishing light. We turned and made our way back to the car park; most of the other cars had left and the roadside café was preparing to close. At Joey's suggestion, I asked them to fill my flask with hot water. It was not a big thing, but in my straightened circumstances, it made both Joey and me feel a little better about our imminent parting of ways. I embraced my friend, turned west and, with the traffic disconcertingly close, began to pick my way along the roadside verge, search for a way to penetrate the adjoining fields and walk the first few miles of my invisible path. Behind me, I heard Joey's warm and cosy car cough and purr as he started to pull away from the car park and, gathering speed, began his journey back south.

---

[10] 'British Camp', Wikipedia. https://en.wikipedia.org/wiki/British_Camp.

Our land was once known as sacred. Something happened that fractured the spiritual tradition that had evolved over thousands of years, signposting the way for the people living on these islands, and also in what we now know as Europe. On many occasions I had come close to following this trail, but something, usually me, got in the way and allowed other, more immediately rewarding enticements to hold sway. All this changed when I began an apprenticeship with a group of Native American healers and teachers, compelling me to confront the depth and breadth of my ignorance about my own land and my own people.

'Name your tribes.'

'Er... what?'

'Name your tribes.'

In no sense was this a request; it was a command. Recognising the familiar, sickening lurch of impending confrontation, sensing the hook's barb working deeper into the soft interior of my open mouth, knowing I am naked before these people, feeling so exposed. What had I spent the endless years at school learning? Surely I knew the answer?

'Your tribes, Mac; name them.'

Feeling abandoned by the gods, my silence admitted failure.

'Iceni, Coritani, Ordovicci, Trinovantes, Brigantes, Atrebates, Silures...'

Even now – and although the tribes are only known to us in their Romanised forms – spoken aloud, the names of our people send bolts of awakening throughout my body and sub-conscious.

'You are English and you are ignorant of your ancestors' tribal history.'

Not a question – a statement of fact.

'Well, actually no...'

Clutching at straws.

'You see, my father was from Northern Ireland, and my mother…'

'Bullshit. You're English.'

Mouth gaping wider, the hook wriggling deeper.

'No, you see, my father…'

'There is something so tedious and predictable about you, Mac.'

No response from me. Better to focus on being the strong and silent type, since opening my mouth wasn't working out too well.

'Tell us. We're curious. How is it that, in all the folk we have met from your islands, not one has admitted to being English? We think you're ashamed of your own people, and that we find… shameful.'

A long pause, as heads turn away, disdaining to see what lives in my eyes.

'Listen, we know about the redcoats, the empire, the colonies, the greedy exploitative trade, the cruel righteousness of the only true way, on and on. We know the whole arrogant story. We know about England, Ireland, Scotland, Wales, and we understand your embarrassment, even shame; but from those islands of yours, all of them, have grown many extraordinary and inspiring freedom fighters. It is disloyal to deny your own land.'

Pause.

'Are you a freedom fighter, Mac?'

Another long pause, but now I am alert; with the heightened awareness of a drowning man, I sense the proximity of shallow water.

'We're sending you out to Lion Rock, Iceni. We're sending you on a vision quest. We're hoping you will remember who you are. You will never be an Indian. You are a Brit. You are Iceni. We can teach you to locate and enter the gateway to your own indigenous past. It will take time; in your case, perhaps, a lot of time. This is our gift. The rest? The rest is up to you.'

Lion Rock is spectacular. Among thousands of hectares of forest, a rock promontory juts out, thrusting itself above a heaving green sea of pinewoods and offering a glimpse of faraway rivers, glades and distant plateaus. Each day I took my place upon the rock and each day I dreamed of my people. Perhaps it seems strange, even antiquated, to be expressing such ideas, but to any indigenous man or woman there would be no raised eyebrows. There is no contradiction in loving all peoples of this world, knowing oneself to be a world citizen, and also knowing the joy of place and tribe. Perhaps the more evolved of us do not have the same resonances; I don't know. I do know, however, that a dog with enough vestigial wolf remembers its family, remembers the old songs and yearns to run to the wild places, blessed of the moon. It is the same with me, and perhaps it is the same with you. On Lion Rock, I found my voice and sang to my people across a continent and across an ocean. And they heard me. How do these things happen? I don't know. You just lean into your longing; you never give up; you never deny the existence of faeries, and you never, ever, lose your sense of humour. And if you do? Well, you just pick yourself up, dust off your trousers, set your cap at a jaunty angle and carry on. Do it fast enough and no one will even notice.

I have grown so fond of ancient history since that time, one of the most important, pivotal eras, an axiomatic time, when the destiny of nations both here and in countless other remote locations around our world hung in the balance, the time when 'civilisation' came to Britain's shores some 2100 years ago. Only recently has this story been retold, in a way that we can hear the wild paean that was once the song of our tribes, the song of our land, the song of belonging.

It is when we are little that we learn to love, or not. What we come to love in early life, what we come to value, is what we later care for. With efficiency and the ruthless pragmatism of repetition, we have been taught that our land only has value insofar as it offers us 'resources'. That most precious substance, repository of incalculable life potential, our soil, is considered 'dirt'. The value of land is seen only in terms of the platform it provides for the building of houses, or the growing of cash crops. For most of 2000 years we have been taught that everything of this earth is dirty, menial and pagan; that is, 'of the country' and therefore inferior. We use language like 'civilisation', 'civilians' and 'civility', Roman-derived words, to describe that which is most desirable: the language of our aspirations; the language of the town- or city-dwellers, nervous of the heathens or 'heath-dwellers', those who preferred freedom and kept covenant with wildness. With the assistance and encouragement of past historians, educators, priests and industrialists, we have lost connection with one of the only things that is literally of true value: our land. We were born from it, we are made of it and, in time, we decompose to become earth once more. So, here in Britain in the twenty-first century, where do we look when we search for spiritual inspiration? To the gurus of India, to the lamas of Tibet, to the shamans of the Americas, to the evangelist ministers of North America or Africa, to the aboriginal peoples of Australia or the Kahunas of the South Seas, to the Tao or Confucius, Islam or Judaism – everywhere but to the direct, tangible, real and impactful experience of our own land; to life. When we lost connection to our land, to the deep intuitive knowing that we belonged to nature, along with all other living beings, we also lost our hearts. Not completely, of course – otherwise we would never have made it even this far – but enough to give us a sense of dislocation, a deep anxiety that expresses itself in an endless bid to possess 'things'. An emptiness that is never satiate for, like the seabirds feeding on the soup of plastic particulates floating in the north Pacific Ocean, it does not nourish us. We feast as we have never feasted before and, with bloated stomachs, we starve to death.

What we once knew, we have forgotten.

***

I found a stile a short way along the road and, taking elaborate care not to slip, I squeezed myself from this world to another. The road was gone, the noise and the smell. Now it was me, a path, a hillside and nothing certain. I had no map, no compass, no tent and no stove. It was the coldest January we had experienced in England for twelve years, and I had several weeks of short days and long nights ahead of me. A little past my prime, I was nevertheless unreasonably confident that, with concentration and application, I could summon my body to assume its erstwhile strength and rise to the occasion. I wanted the excitement of finding my way along the valleys and over the hills that separated me from Mona. I had no idea how easy or difficult it would be. I just knew that my whole being thrilled at the idea of weaving my way through our land, sleeping under a wintry sky, using my resourcefulness and going as deep as I could into the mystery of what my Native American friends called the Black Lodge; winter. This is the dreaming time. In the northern hemisphere, during the winter months the energy of all beings withdraws towards the centre, as the Earth tilts and the seasons change. The light fades and the nights lengthen; temperatures drop and food becomes scarce. Where luxuriant foliage once protected us from unwelcome eyes, now the leaves gaze up from the ground at the great being to whom they owe their brief lives. With what we might imagine as aching loss, they watch colour drain from the landscape and their own forms rupture and tear. At sea, storms surge and swell, racing to meet the land and hurling themselves upon their curving lover. This is the dreaming time. I wanted to go feral, to feel the heat of my animal nature, to know my body in its fierce core. I wanted to dream my way back to my people and sit in council with them. I wanted to experience the warriors' broadswords tearing at my civilised veneer, changing me forever. I wanted to step over the line and leave my old self by a forgotten trackway like a skin cast off. To rot and be consumed by our hungry earth. I wanted to feel desire as I have never known it before. To undress myself and walk naked in the frozen chill of the trees' watery breath. I wanted to dream as our ancestors once dreamt and to know just a little more of what it means to be fully, powerfully, courageously alive.

The path seemed to be taking me northwest, but as the late afternoon light receded, my mind was increasingly focused on finding a place where I could set up camp and stay my first night. I began to hasten, quickening my steps, eyes probing the way ahead, anxious for the relief that would accompany the recognition of a likely spot. Following a small stream along the perimeter of a field and, already experiencing a growing premonition of how significant water would later become to me, I began to gather handfuls of dead herbs and grasses as tinder for the fire that was beginning to occupy all my attention. I could feel the world closing in around me, dark chasing the last rays of light, and a deep quiet settling on the frozen stillness of the surrounding meadows and copses. I stepped off the path and probed a small promontory that thrust itself in the way of the stream. Even in the few hours since I had launched my journey, the world was making sense to me very differently. The dark, the cold, the weight of my backpack, my growing hunger and the knowledge that I needed to prepare properly for this long, cold night all combined to lend me the eyes of the nighttime hunter. I was bent on creating a lair and, if need be, I would defend it. My veneer was peeling away as if it had not been stuck on very well in the first place.

That first night; that first fire. Alone, by the side of a stream, hidden from view, with a carefully prepared sleeping area and long hours ahead of me, I was content. Throughout the journey, I kept a video and audio diary. On listening back to that first night, my voice is thick with weariness and joy as I cook food that I have spent months preparing and offer myself to the deep satisfaction that accompanies any act that is aligned with deep longing. When I wrote *Finding Earth, Finding Soul*, one of the central symbols was the garden. On this journey, I wanted to scale the garden wall, drop down into unknown territory and walk into wildness. For most would-be adventurers, Herefordshire, England is unlikely to be their first choice (unless training with the SAS, who have their regimental headquarters there), but the wild is close – very close. It is the very essence of life, the soul-centre of our joy, the ache that yearns to scream obscenities at everything that is false, pretend and cynical. The wild is everything that our consumerist Christmas is not. It is the heaving, writhing, wetness of sex; the scream accompanying the petite mort; the howl and despair of the grande mort. It is the depth of the fox's amber eye, and the frisson of fear as the owls take up the hunt, sounding their calls and quartering the kill zone. It is the smell of fear and the sound of rain drumming on rock; it is food when you are hungry and water when you are thirsty. It is the fierce pride that lives inside the smallest flame and the pulsing heart of freedom. The heart of freedom. It is the most gentle of caresses and the soul of every kiss freely given. It is my heart. It is the song of these islands, no matter how many millions we are, no matter how long our traffic queues and no matter how dull our jobs. If never before, and if only this, we will know the wild at least twice in our twenty-first-century lives: when we are born and when we die. It can be much, much better than this.

My back resting against a tree and my body warm in my sleeping bag, food in my belly and the comforting ritual of brewing tea. I knew then that fire is the original miracle and that it is truly, magnificently and uncontrollably wild.

Throughout the journey to Mona my night fires became the furnace, heating the crucible of the day past and the night to come. The flames danced for me and I was seduced by their mesmeric candour. They brought the dreams close, like silence spread upon silk.

51 CE, Welsh Border Country

After a decade of humiliation at the hands of a most feared warrior, Ostorious Scapula, Roman Governor of Britain, takes the reins of his horse and silently motions for the XX Legion to move out on patrol. Some miles away, Caractacus, the Catuvellauni chieftain, rides into the hillfort near the goddess shrine of 'All Waters' (Malvern), accompanied by five companions. Dismounting, they duck into one of the roundhouses. Some miles away,

'Caratacus, we cannot delay longer. The Silures want to bring this thing to an end. We are ready!'

All eyes watch the big, calloused hands that warm by the fire. A nursing baby chokes, recovers and eagerly returns to her mother's swollen breast. Lines of tiredness crease the brow of the warrior chief as he reaches out to touch the tiny child's face. His voice is soft, almost a murmur.

'What do you see, dreamer? What do the waters tell us?' From the darkness comes a woman's voice.

'Never a better time and perhaps the last. The people hunger to stand, be seen and fight in the old way. If this belly is not fed, they may act on their own.'

'Two enemies, one cast upon us from beyond Gaul, the other of our own making, *the old way*.' The chief's voice tight, almost sad.

'Caratacus, dearest friend and brother, there is no choice here. The unknowable points the way, the Goddess waters concur. If we decline to stand in open combat with the legions, our tribal alliance with the Silures and Ordovicci will disperse like smoke upon the wind.'

'Then our decision is made. We will stand and take our place. The rest; the rest is a story spoken in blood, prayer and perhaps victory, for those that come after to pick over whatever remains.'

Outside, the early light of dawn creeps upon the sodden hillside and, honking their clan's song, nine wild geese fly west.

The night settles, and my eyelids become heavier. Soon, I will have to release this day and accept the inevitability of the next. I snuggle deeper into my bag and, in the half-formed swirl of images rushing to meet me, I smile silently into the darkness. One part of me prepares to sleep, another, just as vibrant, just as real, prepares to wake. The brain-mind settles and rests; the body-mind slips across the rational border and, in dream state, looks to fly. I sense a falling, a letting-go and the fear-joy of knowing the anchor has broken free. Like the owl that calls, I travel, invisible except to those also asleep, also now moving free in the dream terrain that we mostly only half-remember. Cloud billows, gathers and, like the water it is, heaves over the jagged mountain ridge in a vast cataract, gentling the harsh granite outline of Cwm Silyn. Within the space of one breath, I have gone north a long way. From the earliest age, I have felt the memory of place and people. It is as if the echoes of pain and pleasure, pipe and drums, hopes and fears are stored in the earth and rocks. It is not very comfortable to be born with the songs of extinct animals and forgotten peoples being whispered to you by the torrent of a small stream, or a grey mist drifting across sodden marsh. Ash and oak, willow and hawthorn – they all join in, adding their ancient narrative of hard winters, soft, moist soils and the charcoal burner's axe. It was very confusing and, until I came to the mountains of Eryri[11] it remained a language only half-heard, half-recognised. Having one foot in the twenty-first century, and yet possessing the outlook and sensibilities

---

[11] Snowdonia, North Wales.

of older times in a land where the last wolf probably died in the fifteenth century, makes fitting in difficult. Wolves used to abound in Britain, as did bears, aurochs and lynx. When, from within our warm homes, we hear the scream of a vixen, or even the wailing, rasping and disembodied sounds of domestic cats mating, for a few moments we are reminded of how close the wild is.

Cities can be beautiful, but if beauty is only valued in the language of conventional economics, then no amount of great architectural insight will get us there. For a city to be beautiful, and the people living in that city to remember the true meaning of sacredness, it is necessary to have a sense of geography. London is located on the banks of a great river. It is that great river that makes sense of London; the river is London's great memory and it brings the city alive. When, a few years ago, a whale left the open sea to swim up the Thames to the Houses of Parliament, it brought us a song. It brought us a story. It petitioned our leaders as directly as we who sign our online petitions. That ancient dreamer-whale brought us the song of the wild from the depths of the ocean and delivered it to the seat of government in our country. The Isle of Albion, the White Isle – renamed Britannia by the Romans in the first century CE – received a messenger who carried a petition signed by our unborn children, calling us to pause silently for just one moment, so that we could hear and notice the beating of our own hearts. And it cost the messenger her life.

I cannot dive the depths of the ocean as the whale can, but I can develop and direct other gifts. My soul is archaic. Intuitively, I understand and fancy that I can even speak the old tongue; walk the valleys of this land that have been millions of years in the making and crest the hills that have lifted, tilted and fallen back over more millions of years; walk among the Standing People, the grasses and trees; become softened, gentled, bewildered and the land will speak with us. We have only to make the journey.

Nature will always eventually remind us that she is the alpha and the omega of our earthly existence. The year 2014 began in this way: our January TV screens were filled with images of huge tidal surges battering the southwest coastline of Britain. A succession of storms pirouetted across the Atlantic Ocean and the land was awash. The Somerset levels went underwater as rivers burst banks, and the village of Muchelney became an island marooned. People died, scooped up by waves erupting over breakwaters and sucking those who dared a better view into the chaotic maw of a cold, grey darkness. Alongside the anguished grief of relatives, who grappled with the shock of wild nature reaching into their quiet, normal lives and tearing it apart, there was also something else. As rain lashed the windows of my home and a small stream briefly experimented a route through the front garden, I watched interviews of people who had directly experienced the overwhelming, raw and sometimes devastating impact of the wild, encroaching sea – the landlady of the New Cove Inn, in particular. Animated, smiling, she described the storm, its impact and her prudent retreat to first-floor safety.

'It was frightening in some respects but it was also quite exhilarating. It's just fantastic to watch from up here.'[12]

It was not the inconvenience, anger or dismay that was communicated, but rather delight, excitement, enthralled wonder and awe. I think we crave adventure.

Deeply embedded in the cosmology of many indigenous peoples is a sense of intimate relationship with nature, with the land. There is no disconnection, no concept of separation nor loneliness. Instead, there is a deep sense of kinship with the land, with the Earth, with nature and with each other; a profound knowing of home, of belonging, of inclusion. This worldview is animate; it pulses and breathes and reaches into the very soul of the human. Everything that has physical form,

---

[12] Jackie Brakespeare, 7 January 2014, BBC News at 6pm.

including us, is understood as energy, a spiritual impulse that has briefly assumed a physical presence. The physical form hints at the essence of what is beneath, veiled from casual glance and, to us at least, invisible. Everything is available, but a language has to be learned, along with gratitude, humility and respect. With this comes responsibility. Living in direct relationship with nature, and requiring no reminder of the tribe's reliance on the gifts of nature for food, shelter, tools and clothing, comes a deep and enduring appreciation. Gratitude is of overwhelming importance in many such societies and provides the bedrock upon which the society finds meaning.

I first came across the Kogi Indians through a film by Alan Ereirar, first broadcast on BBC television in 1990.[13] Learning about these people, I found many compelling and deeply thought-provoking insights, but one of their practices had me transfixed. Like most similar societies, their spiritual philosophy is rooted in the animated world within which they live. To the Kogi Indians, the invisible world is the 'real' world; the physical world is its reflection and profound expression. Ceremony, dreaming, divination, deep listening and profound thought fill the world of the Kogi shamans. When a woman becomes pregnant, it is, of course, an event of great significance for the tribe. The shamans gather and, with infinite care, divine whether or not the unborn child is a shaman. If it is concluded that this is the case, then the woman takes up residence deep inside a ceremonial cave. The place chosen within the cave is sufficiently deep into the cliff to exclude almost all light. Here, in the dark-shadowed mystery of the cave, in the womb of Mother Earth, the woman gives birth.

Almost no light; just enough to allow the eyes of the infant to develop properly.

Almost no scent; except, perhaps, the very occasional diluted whiff of an unknown outside world.

---

[13] *The Heart of the World: Elder Brother's Warning* (dir. Alan Ereirar), BBC, first broadcast 1990.

No colour; even the food is chosen for its pale colour once the baby is weaned.

Almost no sound; only the mother and those others caring for the child. No sound of wind, rain, birds, the village or animals.

Cave walls, losing themselves in the ancestor's shadows, perhaps the muted splash of water poured from a gourd. No forest, no parakeets, no muffled jaguar growl, no birdsong and no water dripping like honey from wet leaves. No green, no damp smell of earth and decaying vegetation, no sunshine, no sunrise, no sunset and no clouds. None of this, yet plenty of love, play and interaction with caring elders who teach the mystery of the Kogi way.

Years pass – nine in total. Then, one day, having spent the entirety of his or her young life in the soft darkness of the mountain womb, the child is turned towards the cave entrance and begins a journey towards the light. Beams of sunlight move like a lover's touch across the cave floor, sounds incomprehensible to young ears echo, rise, fall and beckon. All manner of scents insinuate the cave tunnels, tantalising, wondrous; a sensuous feast awaits.

One step further. The child stands at the threshold of the cave and looks out onto the world.

It is said that they never recover. *Never* recover. Never recover from the beauty.

For a whole life, the shaman then walks among the people, reminding them of that which has been so freely and generously shared; the chance of a life on the Earth. The opportunity to taste, touch, see, smell, feel, luxuriate and relish the glorious, fecund, astounding and prodigious truth of this that we call *ordinary*.

What is ordinary? A place that I can call home, where I will find good food, clean water, warmth, light and safety? A national health system, born three years after 'Little Boy' hurtled out of the sky and decimated Hiroshima, killing in excess of 129,000 people? What is ordinary? Beaches where we can swim in the sea, play with our children and picnic together? Gardens that we can tend, growing flowers and vegetables? Smartphones, aeroplanes, restaurants, movies, theatres, television and health spas? National parks, civil rights and political rights? Free schooling and libraries? Sunrise, sunset, the moon, sky, clouds, rain, the wind and the ocean? Friendship, lovers, sex, husbands, wives, families, music, art and each other? Whatever our preferences, there is nothing 'ordinary' about the ordinary. This word that we use to describe the commonplace carries a contempt that, viewed from the Kogi Indians' perspective, should leave us slack-jawed at our ignorant indifference and profound ingratitude. Held within the ordinary is the full breadth and sweep of William Blake's vision, Shakespeare's sonnets, Nelson's leadership, Pankhurst's activism or Boudica's standard. It is the only true Holy Grail and is available every moment of every day, have we only the wit to see it.

The Kogi Indians offer us a hard mirror. We, as Oscar Wilde quipped:

'... know the price of everything and the value of nothing.'[14]

Somewhere along the beaten trail we lost some things of value, including our humility and deep appreciation for this priceless Earth. Such carelessness. What makes it all the more pathetic is the frantic, obsequious, beseeching, desperate pleading we so often exhibit when confronted with imminent death. The willingness to do almost anything to stay the moment of no return and win even just a few minutes more of this 'valueless' life. If we did not know it before, we certainly know appreciation when, like the coiled garden hose, it dribbles, drips and stops. The land is in our blood, in our aching sexuality, in our yearning and in all of our best ideas. The land can ease our incipient madness and bring us into relationship. All scents of earth – wood smoke, forest, green leaf and water – stimulate earliest memories that speak of home. The path behind is strewn with discarded and

---

[14] Oscar Wilde, 'Lady Windermere's Fan, A Play About a Good Woman', first performed February 1892.

disregarded gems, once known as sacred. Like our songs, our stories, our celebration of the seasons and the thresholds that all humans make as they advance through a lifetime. Alongside bracken, docks, couch grass, dandelions and nettles, sycamore trees, grey squirrels, rats, wolves, youth, new age travellers and immigrants we endlessly uphold our virtuous, scrubbed and self-righteous world. The list of the unwelcome sweeps up all those plants, animals and human beings that we identify as weeds, vermin, alien species, undesirables – all that speaks of wildness. That which threatens the mowed lawn; that which we cannot control. The wild. And yet, the further we sanitise and ostracise, the lonelier we feel, and the more fearful we become. In losing the land, we are in danger of losing our soul.

A Yankunytjatjara elder and a traditional keeper of Uluru, Tjilpi[15] (more widely known as Uncle Bob Randall), visited Embercombe with Sophia Latham in 2006. Sophia was assisting Tjilpi in the screening of *Kanyini*, an award-winning film about his experience as one of the 'stolen generation', mixed-race aboriginal children who were snatched from their families and 'educated' as whites.[16]

Under the rusting corrugated iron roof of the mission schoolroom, the newly named young Bob Randall laboured to learn. His missionary teachers were strange people, he told us. During the day they would rant and rave about the evils of the flesh and the purity of God's only son, but when it got dark, some of them fell silent. Many of Bob's friends were summoned in the nighttime and were obliged to submit to 'special treatment'. One stifling afternoon, the kids were sat at their desks as usual, each one absorbed in trying to draw the Bible that sat upright and open at the front of the class. Sat by the classroom window, a child was drawing something different. He had begun to draw the Bible, but a different image had inserted itself into his mind's eye and demanded form. His

---

[15] An honorific title signifying eldership.
[16] *Kanyini* (dir. Michelle Hogan), 2006.

pencil scratched the thin paper as he outlined a boat. Absorbed, intent, he allowed the image to settle on the page, and never saw the teacher loom close until it was too late.

'What's that?'

Excited, breathless. 'It's a boat. It…' Ominous, jagged, menacing.

'I can see it's a boat. That is *not* what I told you to draw.'

The boy, still overwhelmed with his inner knowing, exclaims: 'It's on its way. It'll be here in a few days!'

He was beaten for this, dragged to the front of the class and beaten with all the ferocious anger of the frightened and ignorant.

Tjilpi said, 'It was normal for us, the land speaking. It was our Kanyini, our connectedness. Normal for us to know things before we saw them; before they happened. Nobody thought twice about it. It was just the way the world is, beautiful, loving, connected.'

Three days later, in view of the classroom, the first boat to arrive in years pulled in to the bay; a very beautiful white yacht. We had this once – we, too, once had our Kanyini. It never went away, but rather faded from our vision, became invisible and, like breath, was inhaled back into the land. Sometimes, we chance upon it, catching a fleeting glimpse from the corner of an unfocused eye, feel it through the soles of our feet and, in moments of lucid wakefulness, when our mental illness briefly subsides, we touch close to the truth held to our lips like a glass of spring water. With long periods in nature, and intimate with life, the visceral wild will reassert itself. Prescience becomes familiar again, the subtlety of life's vast vocabulary. We sat by fires with Tjilpi, cooking wild meat in the way of his people. He spoke about Kanyini, the twin energy streams; the four principles of Ngura, a sense of belonging to home and land; Walytja, family connecting with life; Kurunpa, love, spirit and soul; and Tjuukurpa, knowing creation and the way of right living. He spoke about the tragedy that befell his people when my culture cut each of these life-connecting threads. He spoke about his people's exile as they wandered in the netherworld in limbo, a people adrift. For a great number of his people's young, sniffing petrol is all that is left. We are not so different, of course. We snort, drink, inject, ingest and smoke anything that will keep us safely numb. We call it entertainment. We, too, walk sightlessly; we, too, dream of something more beautiful than this. Tjilpi never relinquished hope. Courageously, he chose to walk the long path; singing, storytelling, campaigning, writing and loving his way home. For his own people, he pointed a way, but he was even more generous than this. His love of life embraced us also. He could see that our Kanyini had also been cut. He knew that we all have to walk home together, that no one should be left behind.

I met Tjilpi once more before his death on 13 May 2015, when I was speaking at the Uplift Festival in Byron Bay, Australia. As one of the custodial elders of Uluru,[17] and as a man who had campaigned tirelessly for his people's rights, many loved Tjilpi. We met a few days before the festival. Holding each other's hands, he looked at me with eyes that reminded me of my mother's when, at a similar stage in her life, she felt the tug of source calling her back. In old age a few short months can make a big difference, and I could see that he was close to letting go.

There was a retraction, a kind of pulling-back; the ancestors felt close.

Day 2: Saturday, 3 January

I awoke to darkness. The dreams had slipped away, as shadows melting before the encroaching dawn. The mystery of the night

---

[17] Also known as Ayers Rock, Uluru is a land of profound spiritual significance to aboriginal Australians.

before surrendered to my mind's insistence on turning to face the day. I was excited, apprehensive and joyful.

The route I chose to walk was, for the most part, made on the basis of two sets of data – the first being the two stars that I had identified, the sun and Polaris, which could offer me reliable information; the other being whatever I could see in my immediate environs at any given time. Over a period of weeks, I would take thousands of small navigational decisions, some of which would be helpful to my overall aim, and some less so. However, much of the time I would not have any idea of where I was; even after the journey's end I would only have a very general idea of the route I had travelled. While I loved the idea of travelling blind, I did also relish the idea of later studying the impact of my decisions and their relevance to my progress. On top of this, I anticipated, one day, retracing my steps by car and trying to find the remains of my campfires, knowing that, although they might have become less visible, they would still exist, softly imprinted on the yielding earth. So, within my kit was a small GPS device that, when switched on, would triangulate my position and deliver a set of numbers as two five-figure co-ordinates, providing an accurate Ordnance Survey grid reference. Given the forecasted sub-zero temperatures, my lack of focused preparation and the less-than-convincing impression I gave of robust fitness, I had agreed to text the co-ordinates to my former wife, Azul. In this way, I would provide the information that would be necessary for someone to locate me if I found myself in extremis. At the time, these sets of figures were of no relevance to the choices I made, but it was comforting to know that, one day, in a more comfortable future, I could unfold a map and, with a cup of steaming tea in hand, trace this wintry journey.

My stick lay on the ground where I had positioned it the night before as I gazed at the heavens through the brittle lacework of bare tree limbs. It pointed north. The previous afternoon, following Joey's departure, I had walked only three miles before the sun dipped below the horizon, and I was left peering into the dark somewhere west of the Malvern Hills. After getting the fire going again and munching some venison jerky and a few handfuls of dried apple, I broke camp. I could deduce from the valley contours that a river most likely lay to the north, so for the first few kilometres I chose footpaths that took me southwest and towards higher ground. Emotionally, I was on a rollercoaster, lurching between moments of sublime tranquillity and raw, wrenching tenderness. I felt so happy to be free, alive and living an adventure, but with each forward step came an intimation of challenges yet to come. Passing by the occasional cottage, I noticed that this was Audi country. Almost every other parked car was testament to the brand, design and sales genius of some nearby dealership and the comfortable, well-heeled status of most local residents. Snippets of conversation followed my passage, with one gentleman asking me where I was going and, having established that I did not know, running after me brandishing a map. It was a very confusing interchange, particularly for my new friend, who observed that I kept averting my eyes from the map, while clearly stating that I had no idea where I was, or where I was planning to sleep the night. It could have become embarrassing, but, somehow, we both chose to ignore my peculiar behaviour and focus instead on the weather; a topic that had both of us bemused, uncertain and irrationally hopeful.

A grey, leaden sky squatted over the pretty countryside as I trudged on. Mile followed mile, and for the first time I began to enjoy the rhythm of my footfall and the tapping of my stick. I began to have an intimation of walking into a deeper presence with the land and with myself. It reminded me of so many past ceremonies when, fasting, I would need to re-orientate myself to the pulse of something initially indefinable and hard to identify. A cadence, obscured by the pattern of days, designed to the demands of our voracious market economy and not so much the circling breath of my older, animal self. I was walking in what was probably the southernmost reach of Dobunni tribal territory. By all accounts, they seem to have offered no resistance to Rome, following the calculating example of their powerful neighbours in the east, the Catuvellauni, and welcoming the economic benefits that co-operation with the empire brought. There exist tantalising remnants of information that might suggest other, less-calculating preoccupations in the Dobunni's guardianship of the sacred hot springs at Bath, and the existence of a 'raven clan', from which Worcester's older name of Branogena derives. My path was also taking me close to the northeastern border of the Silures, a tribe whose land pretty much corresponds to the South Wales valleys. The Silures were not enamoured of Rome, and so aligned with the resistance leader, Caratacus, in his famous humiliation of Rome's best, further developing their reputation as a fiercely independent people and highly skilled warriors. A reputation that has endured longer in the stories and songs of the people than the tribe's name, which eventually became hidden in language describing a geological era, the Silurian – the third period of the Palaeozoic.

My reverie was abruptly interrupted, as I suddenly became aware of the approaching dusk. It was to take a few days before I was able to simultaneously juggle the pressing needs of my physical welfare with the dreams and feelings that erupted, unbidden, into my consciousness. Throughout my journey, finding a place to bivouac was not a simple undertaking. For long stretches, I would not see any houses and those that I did see were often bounded by small private gardens. The thousands of acres of woodland, scrub, fields and wetlands were no doubt owned by someone, but by whom? And where would I find them to ask permission? And why should I ask permission? Whose land is this? Can land be owned? To my mind it was not simple, either practically or philosophically. Added to this, my time for walking was doubly constrained by the hours of light, and the amount of effort and time it took to provide myself with a hot drink, hot food and a good stock of firewood for the evening. With no stove, and carrying a very limited supply of water, I was obliged to look for places where I had access to both. Very aware of how precious was the battery life of my head torch, and exhausted by the end of each day, I became focused in my search for a lair. Wherever I chose, should the owner become aware of my presence, they might not like a vagrant, displaced Iceni treating the place as his own. In any case, since, for the most part, asking permission seemed utterly impractical and possibly complicated, I resolved to go feral and hide myself away from unwelcome eyes. With every mile I was rapidly shedding the unhelpful niceties of obedience to laws that seemed unfairly weighted to the advantage of the few, and that were separating me from a pathway calling. Requiring only a few dead sticks, a trickle of water from a hedgerow gulley, and the safety of remaining undisturbed during the hours of darkness, in my straightened circumstances my needs seemed well within the hospitable instincts of any half-reasonable person.

No water in my flask and no stream in sight; no accessible woodland and daylight fast receding. Living on Britain's west coast, with as much water as I could ever possibly desire or need, it had never occurred to me that I would find myself experiencing the first waves of panic at the prospect of no water to drink. It was now dark and I could see very little. In the gloom, I noticed a small lane going south and up a hill. I was very tired, dehydrated and cold, but I was also fixated on the image of a small, warm fire, some chapattis and lying horizontal on a bed of soft leaves. The lane shifted angle and became steeper. My breath became more laboured, and my eyes darted to either side, looking for the combination of features that might promise a home for the night. Impenetrable, steep-sided banks blanketed in bramble, a muddy ditch and the lane continuing its uncaring, upward passage. Another fifteen minutes passed and I was losing faith. Then, as the lane took another curve to the right, it abruptly finished at the gates of some kind of property, perhaps an estate; too posh for a farm. Either side of the gates was a copse of woodland sufficiently big for me to create a hide and secrete myself away for the night. The backpack thumped on to the ground and I began to look for a way into the woodland. The sky had cleared, and a canopy of stars blessed the shriek of a vixen as she began the night's work. As I was standing, looking into the wood, taking advantage of the moonlight to see where I might gain access, something drew my gaze to the left, and there, crouched to avoid detection, I saw the silhouette of a man stalking me. I gave no sign that I had observed his presence, and allowed my gaze to traverse across the wood's boundary, as if I were still taking in my surroundings. With the moon behind him, I realised that he did not know that his position was compromised. From the corner of my eye, I saw him very slowly and deliberately slip between the long cathedral pillars of the pine forest and take up a new position, still watching. Softly, I held him in my peripheral vision, not wishing him to feel the penetrating energy of eyes that locate like the sights of a rifle. It is a very strange, exhilarating and intimidating feeling when you know that you are being hunted. I had no reason to think that he wished me harm, but there was, nevertheless, a silent, implied animosity in his concealment and stealth. In the weeks to come, I can well imagine that others perceived me in this way, as I waited for dark before lurching out of the shadows and, clinging to anonymity, ran for the location I had identified as promising shelter and concealment. The short, frozen days; the long, dark nights; the ever-present history of a people who had defended and then lost everything; the deliberate, focused intention of seeking and accessing hidden gateways that would bring me closer to my heart; the weight and bulge of the Iceni chariot ring in my pocket. With each passing day, each campfire, each hour, each cup of water, I was descending into a netherworld, from which the earliest days have always beckoned the memory of sacredness.

> Like one who, on a lonely road,
> Doth walk in fear and dread,
> And, having once turned round, walks on,
> And turns no more his head;
> Because he knows a frightful fiend
> Doth close behind him tread.[18]

---

[18] Samuel Taylor Coleridge, 'The Rime of the Ancient Mariner', 1798, Part 1, Verse 450.

Striving to maintain a sense of his location, I could feel that he was moving, yet staying nearby. A shadow swallowed the silhouette, as a cloud passed in front of the moon and I lost him. Bending to my backpack and pulling out some warmer clothing, I considered my choices. I did not feel safe here. As soon as I had built my fire, I would be illuminated and the surrounding darkness more profound. I pulled the straps tight and shouldered my pack. Then, turning back the way I had come, I began walking back down the hill and around the first curve of the lane, until I was out of sight. Without pausing, I switched my torch off and quickly jogged another 200 metres. Still; listening and watching. Time became suspended as I waited and watched, all senses probing the way I had come. Slowly, I began to relax and consider my situation. I was even more thirsty, very tired and still without a place to rest and sleep. I did not see the field gate until I almost collided with it. Trying to manage my rising excitement, I raised the latch and squeezed through, carefully and silently closing it behind me. It was like walking into another world. I found myself on a rounded hillside promontory, with a panorama of stars off to the north, and a thick, banked, uncut hedge between the lane and me. It was not a cosy site, but it felt safe; there was lots of dry wood, and somehow the hillside had an uplifting quality. Making fire was always very intense. I would make detailed preparations, gathering tiny piles of twigs, sorted by size, and then a much larger stash of small branches to cook by and keep me company. With darkness arriving by 4.30pm, the nights were very long and very cold. My fires became the very soul of my journey, the whispered presence of ancient relatives. I was committed to this place, but I still lacked water. So, again, alert to the necessity of keeping my hideout's location hidden, I retraced my path back to the gate, out on to the lane, then started walking short distances, stopping and listening intently. In retrospect, it was largely due to this constant preoccupation with listening, intuiting, sensing and tracking that I fell into a deeper relationship with the transient, phantom being that is our true essence. I learned more about presence during January of

2009 than at any time previously. I also reached much deeper into gratitude. During the third foray into silence, I heard the sound that I was seeking: the slightest gurgle and swish of a rivulet, hidden among the decaying leaves of the ditch. Ten uncomfortable minutes later, with knees yelling their discomfort and an ominous crunch in my lower back, I had my water filtered and into the flask. I was happy.

Some hours later, revelling in the peace and majesty of a spectacular winter night sky, and toasted by a fire that held me enraptured, I stood and looked up to the Great Bear, tracing my way to the North Star. I turned and faced northwest, arms flung to the horizon. Somewhere out there, across swaths of hills and valleys, frigid with cold and bathed by the Celtic Sea, lay Mona, birthplace of my reawakening.

59 CE, summer, the Isle of Mona, mystery school of the druids

On the far shore, a rider breaks cover from the woodland and urges her horse down to the beach. The boatman glances over his shoulder to the distant island and receives the acceptance signal just as the horse and rider swerve to a standstill, panting, sweating and quivering with urgency. No word is spoken as the boat swings out into the slack water and the oars dip to their task. Thirty minutes later, and now more composed, Namahea speaks to the dreamers.

'Gaius Suetonius Paulinus is in Britain, his bloody business in the desert kingdom done. Our spies say he looks to Mona.'

Softly, the returning voice measures the news. 'Ah, so it is come at last.'

'The Ordovices will not hold long without the Silures, and Paulinus is an order of brutality beyond all others. We must prepare for the unthinkable.'

Tiny wavelets stroke the seashore as the tide begins its slithering return. Thoughts, fears and imaginings jostle in the jagged silence. 'Call the elder council. It is to Hibernia[19] we must look now. Namahea, what of the girl child, the one who never forgets? We know she lives but time grows short and the Eagle scours the land for her footprints.'

'The Fox makes his way to the Dumnonii, who hold her in safekeeping. They will hasten her to Mona but mostly under cover of darkness. The Eagle is blind once the sun goes down.'

'It may be so, brave sister, but the Dobunni trackers they enlist are not. Hold her safe to your heart. The gods be willing, she is the one who will sing the ocean ceremony when the boat leaves Mona.'

Day 3: Sunday, 4 January

I awoke, limbs aching and stiff, but in good spirits. The cold was intense. Just before leaving my camp, I poured myself a cup of water, only to find that it had developed a film of ice just a few minutes later. Ever since the first walk around Embercombe's perimeter, the weight of the pack on my hips had been cause for concern. After this first reality check, I had reduced my pack's weight to something in the region of 65 lbs (29.5 kg), but two days into my journey it still felt too heavy. Contemplating the endless hours of growing my field of wheat, leaching tannins from my acorns and all the accumulated effort this represented, I was resistant to the inevitable conclusion. I pressed on. The previous day, road signs had indicated that I was on my way into Hereford and, hemmed in by a river to the north and rising land to the south, I could not avoid going through the town. A footpath contoured around the hillside, taking me south-southwest and, weighing my options, this seemed a reasonable compromise.

---

[19] The ancient Roman name for Ireland.

I arrived in Hereford around 4pm, like a shadow, unseen, a wraith gliding, as a memory of otherness among the New Year bargain hunters who were thronging the streets. Self-conscious, very tired and, by now, increasingly worried about my health, I was bent over with pain and keen to retrieve the quiet solace of my lone path. With daylight fading, I thankfully escaped the town and began heading out, past a school and some playing fields. My heart lightened at the prospect of a fire and sleep, but I was also aware that I again needed to replenish my water flask. Only just beyond Hereford's outskirts and unable to find water, I decided to knock on the door of a farmhouse. It was now very dark. I had not washed for several days and I looked as I felt – and, no doubt, also smelt. With some misgivings, and pondering whether my condition and request might seem a little odd, I opened the farm gate, went to the door and knocked rather louder than I had intended. Voices sounded and a porch light illuminated my plight, before the front door opened and an elixir of warmth, home, baking and light flooded my being.

'I'm very sorry to bother you, but I need some water. Do you have an outside tap I could use?'

She looked uncommonly beautiful. A kind, open and unafraid face, framed in golden hair, appraised my condition and request.

'Come in, my dear, you look as if you could do with a little more than just water.'

Any thoughts of 'Are you sure?' and 'Well, if it's not too much trouble' were flung aside as I shed my pack, struggled through the door and entered another world. Overcome with gratitude, and aware that I looked quite incongruous in my new surroundings, I began to mutter something about not wishing to intrude, but my host brushed aside my protestations and took me into the living room.

'Here, Mum, we have a guest.'

A very elderly lady sat in front of the TV on a sofa. Craning to see me, she patted the cushion beside her, as I positively answered questions about cake, biscuits, sandwiches and a hot cup of tea. Without pause, I just said 'yes' to everything. Mum was watching the iconic and controversial movie adaptation of Shakespeare's *King Lear*, directed by Peter Brook and starring Paul Scofield. Pressed into each other, mouth crammed with cake and beginning to sweat profusely, I found myself almost immediately in a conversation about the great actor and his burgeoning talent, sombre dignity and cadaverous portrayal of Lear's descent into madness. The world of this production is bleak, terrifying and cruel. It helped me to put things into perspective.

I found the kindness and generosity of my new friends very moving. This encounter, along with many, many others, gave me countless uplifting insights into the care and humanity of most people. How we interact and welcome strangers must surely be an important measure, providing insight into the values and mores of a society. All too soon, every creative effort to prolong my indulgence had been exploited and, in any case, all the cake having been eaten, Lear's agony was beginning to take its toll on my improved wellbeing. Resolving to one day return and thank my hosts properly, I tilted into the night again and became swallowed by the freezing darkness. It is challenging walking blind, keeping company with yourself and trusting that the darkness will yield to your needs. The track led me through a small thicket of hedgerow and wasteland, before abruptly arriving at a main road. I retraced my steps and explored my options with eyes increasingly confident and skilful at spotting opportunities for a comfortable bivouac. Another fire was kindled into being, and I submitted to an overweening sense of being cared for and guided. I felt embraced, thankful and wealthy beyond measure. I was only a few metres from the public footpath, hidden behind a fallen tree, yet, checking the camp's visibility by crossing a ditch and regaining the path, my location was almost completely concealed from view. Only the scent of wood smoke would have alerted most passers-by. I slept easy, my head close to the small, leaping flames of a willow fire.

Dawn was still some hours away when I woke to the unpleasant realisation that, warm and snug as I was, I needed to piss. With focused concentration, I searched for the toggle, attempted the delicate task of unzipping the sleeping bag without snagging it and, eventually, reluctantly emerged to the frigid embrace of a deep frost. Eyes drifted skyward and the panoply of stars wrapped me in awe. Petty thoughts of inconvenience were left to float ghostlike among the trees, dispossessed and bereft of power. A handful of sticks cast on the glowing embers and flames leapt hungrily to their task. I wriggled back into my cocoon. Once more drowsy, happy for the shadows playing across my face and the crackle of heat and cold dancing with each other, still hypnotised by the stars, I surrendered to dreams.

Waves lap on some distant shore. The waxing crescent moon glides through the immensity of a great darkness. Out beyond, somewhere, I hear the bark of a dog. Words spoken by the Kogi Indians swoop towards me.

'What is the purpose of a human life? To care for all living things. What else?'

It is the incorruptible sanity, the peace and compassionate surrender to life in this simple assertion that tears at the temptation to compromise. If, upon this principle of love, we undertook the design of our schools, colleges and universities, what might we create together? It is not easy to witness the world as it is. To avoid nothing and, without circumvention, stand close to the truth, scorched by the horror of our cruel indifference. I see the transcendent beauty of human beings and I see the malignant ignorance that triumphs in desecration. We seem so full of fear, so shamed, so terrified of living as life invites us to live. Located outside their homes and places of spiritual practice, Tibetan Buddhists have, for many centuries, placed brightly coloured flags as prayers offered to the wind;

the flags' vibrant colours, their movement and sound as they snap and fold to the wind's fierce teaching; the vast landscape of mountain and sky, like waves retreating before the tide; the tireless messages of wild love spoken to a world beyond by troops of colour, suspended and weightless in the blue light of the garden planet. Each day, as I walked footpaths, tracks, paths, lanes and roads, I saw our prayer flags. They spoke truly about our gods and goddesses. They faithfully represented a societal contempt and indifference for everything outside and beyond our brief, fleeting and very partial pleasure. I do not think that I exaggerate, inflate or otherwise distort; I report what I see.

The trail of fires that accompanied my pathway through the hills and valleys of this blessed land were strewn with garbage. Almost without break, continuously throughout the entire journey, my attention would be wrested towards the crass artwork of branded soft drinks, confectionary wrappers and the discarded mugs, cartons and bags of assorted fast food outlets. We have even exported the same to Tibet, hence the rubbish dump that is the Everest base-camp. Recalling the words of Psalm 121, 'I lift up mine eyes unto the hills, from whence cometh my help', on so many countless occasions I would see a plastic bag caught in the hedgerows, flapping and billowing its desolate, disconnected story.

The moon fades as I drift and sleep. It is the contempt that I find hard.

Day 4: Monday, 5 January

Every day grew colder, and every day took me some steps deeper into mystery. For some miles, I followed a Roman road, increasingly aware that I was moving through an area that had once been a borderland between lowland and upland Britain, and strategically important at many times in history. With the second-largest Iron-Age hillfort to the north of Credenhill and Magnis, a Roman town, to the south, it took very little to feel the relationship between land and place. The River Wye was close by, and as my boots beat their monotonous rhythm upon the tracks and lanes, I knew I was walking shoulder-to-shoulder with the legions, as supplies and troops cautiously marched this beautiful and contested ground. Hidden in a little wood and now, somehow, feeling the measure of my undertaking, I slept with a light heart.

Day 5: Tuesday, 6 January

My trail of fires bit deeper into the country as I pressed on towards the northwest. I had imagined that this journey would primarily focus upon nature, the land and a world less populated by human beings; in fact, it was not like that. The valleys, the woodland, the streams, birds, ice, animals and all forms of our wild, parallel world were indeed close, but I had never expected such kindness from so many people. Cars drew up alongside me as I walked and offered me lifts; unbidden strangers hailed me, made enquiry and offered their assistance. Once, after having passed me in his car, a man returned with a weather report advising me to seek accommodation, as the temperature was forecasted to dip below $-7°C$. One kindly couple stopped on two separate occasions, offering me a hot drink and counselling a less-arduous interpretation of my mission. Countless encounters with people of all kinds gave expression to generosity, kindness, humour and hospitality. With one notable exception, this was true over the entirety of my journey. For some miles on the fifth day, I walked with a very upright, courteous and dignified man who turned out to be a retired nuclear submarine commander. He told me that I had been observed walking out of Hereford, and various ex-military friends of his had noted my presence. Their assumption had been that I was with 'the regiment' – the SAS. It seems that, with my face obscured, I did not appear quite as frail as I had imagined. Buoyed with this information my stride lengthened and for a while, at least, I felt thirty years younger.

As if banked into steeper waves by a huge wind, the land began to rise and dip more steeply. The softly undulating apple-growing landscape of Hereford and the thick bunches of mistletoe adorning many of the trees gave way to narrow inclines and a more vaunted, primal atmosphere; I was entering Ordovices territory. As the land heaved and swelled, so I, too, found myself more sure-footed – my task emblazoned in the wild heart of my longing, my soul-memory reaching for home. Each and every bivouac gave me a unique experience. Scratch my surface and I was an animal emerging from hibernation. When I chose, I became invisible and found, at last, the experience for which I was searching. Others before me made this journey.

After Caratacus' defeat, the subjugation of the Silures and Ordovices and the invasion of Mona, the legions still failed to ever fully pacify the British tribes west of the line running from the Severn Estuary to the Humber. Yet, still people took the risk to travel. How many, I wonder, found themselves concealed in the gullies and crags of this land, before risking unwelcome encounters with Roman patrols and heading for distant Mona. Arriving at Norton, I crossed to the north side of the river and, gingerly negotiating a steep meadow, found a densely wooded hillside away from the public footpath where I could hunker down for the night. The identification of my hideouts would herald a surge of emotions. Living so intimately with the history of this land, I felt that I viewed everything from the other side of a gauze curtain. The land I occupied was truly wild, holding danger and safety alike. A stick snapping under my careless foot could alert a hidden foe and send me softly to the ground as, ears straining, I waited and listened. Under the fir trees, I would level a small corridor of ground, heaping the soft comfort of richly aromatic leaf litter, careful to orientate myself to gain a view of the moon through the canopy. A tiny fire swiftly lit using birch bark, and then twenty minutes gathering a stash of wood sufficient to take me through my evening led me, heavy lidded, submitting to sleep.

By the time I reached Norton, my interest in food was diminishing. In my wearied condition, it took a lot of effort to manage the pan, water, fire and foodstuffs. I would find myself making chapattis and chewing some apple or deer meat before, thankfully, stretching out in front of the fire. I was aware that a growing disinterest in food did not necessarily combine very well with long, physically demanding days and very cold weather, but past experience had taught me that I could go a long time without food if necessary and, in many ways, enjoy it.

Each fire-lit night I would unfold into a somatic dreamscape; the crackle and heat of the fire; the smoke curling and weaving like water in a stream; the screech of owl or bark of fox. The Iceni chariot ring held to the dark sky, alive and pulsing in hands deeply oak-tanned from innumerable fires, and my dreaming stone bathed in springs, streams and lakes, describing the small, sacred centre with which I would pray. Gratefully resting my back against one of the trees, and perching above the homes of this lovely village, I travelled back to earlier times, remembering my instructions. Looking back now, I know I was graced. Archetypes derived from ancient memory, ephemera that dwell in the between places, shafts of perspective that illuminate the numinous and moments of conscious awareness when I know that I am being spoken to have always been alive and present in my life, as real as stone is real. The challenge has been in trusting what is real, when the prevailing and relentlessly dismissive story of our time condemns the imaginal soul-knowing of our ancient lineage, earned and fashioned over millennia. Only regular and frequent touching into this world allows it to survive the blunt and ponderous weight of mind that permits no deviant thoughts of freedom, flight, or otherness. Alone in the copse, I had no such constraints.

Thirty years ago, among the mountains of Snowdonia and together with some dear friends, I responded to a call and leant into the magic of mountains that resonate, still, to an older drum. We took some substantial risks and might have paid dearly for the privilege, but I believe that, in some way I do not understand, we were protected. We undertook dreaming journeys that carved a fealty with soul torn from a small child's pining entreaty, 'Is this all?' I made a pact at this time, swivelling the dial on my compass, snapping it shut and looking to the horizon. The bright path led me to this copse.

60 CE, the Isle of Mona

Suetonius Paulinus' legions attack the island and begin the slaughter. A dreamer lies hidden, buried in Mona's soft earth and holding a small child close, as the legionnaires search for survivors to mutilate and kill.[20]

'They are close; very close. I smell them. I have seen what none of Mona should see. I have seen our peoples' dreams trampled, and the destiny of countless generations blighted by the ignorance and hubris of a depraved emperor whose hatred of others is only matched by his fear of death.

Hush, hush, little one, make no sound. Here, look in to my eyes. They are dark, like the ocean, like the night, like the ceremony cave, where first I brought you into this world. Now, let us hold silence, for I feel the cold breath of Rome standing above us and I fear to hear your screams, should they find us and be shamed by your soft beauty.

With the power of my dreaming body I reach beyond and call you, soldier. You think it's your own mind working, your own thoughts. That is as well. Move away from the tree, feel the pull of my mind's eye; let these two rocks remind you of your lover's thighs twined around your waist and call you to explore. Yes, that's right; that's good. Waste yourself on phantom dreams of my creation. Between us, I breathe a cloak that masks what should not be seen.'

---

[20] The term 'dreamer' is here attributable to Manda Scott and her compelling *Boudica* novels.

That night, as I huddled closer to the comforting radiance of my fire, and peered into caverns of glowing flame-gold, I contemplated brutality.

I was educated to believe that Rome was a good thing for Britain. The art historian, broadcaster and museum curator Sir Roy Strong served to bolster that belief with statements of this kind:

> Britain was only one of many countries which suffered the consequences of the collapse of the Roman Empire. In England's case the effect was far more dramatic, for there was no continuity as two-thirds of the eastern part of the island passed into the hands of the German, pagan, and illiterate warrior tribesmen. Urban society collapsed, and the Latin language was abandoned in favour of British or primitive Welsh.[21]

This story of Rome's beneficence and cultural sophistication has been touted as fact for decades; vague assertions of the hideous, barbaric practices of the druids in particular, and of our tribal ancestors in general, have been mostly accepted as an embarrassing truth. Thankfully, the mist is clearing somewhat, and although we were no doubt as bloodthirsty as our Gaullish and German neighbours, it would be a tough challenge indeed to trump Rome when it came to unbridled, cultivated and systemic savagery. Hunting foxes with hounds does not really compare as a blood sport to the Emperor Nero's fondness for nailing Christians to stakes, tarring and torching them and then using the light they shed to illuminate his garden parties – their screams as background music. Furthermore, the civilisation that so ingeniously built a military juggernaut, the like of which the world had never seen before, was led by many commanders who redefined the meaning and experience of 'necessary force' for our ancestors.

---

[21] Roy Strong, *The Spirit of Britain: A Narrative History of the Arts* (Hutchinson/Pimlico, London, 1999), p. 22.

By his own account, and on just one particular occasion, in 55 BCE, Julius Caesar massacred 430,000 German tribespeople who had come to him seeking asylum, most of them women and children. The Roman Senate responded by decreeing a celebration for this momentous victory.[22]

Earlier that year Caesar had exterminated two other German tribes, killing around 150,000 people, when they entered what is now the Netherlands, having been displaced from their traditional lands by rival neighbouring tribes.[23] This was Rome's unquestioning commitment to 'might is right' – their adherence to a similar belief emerging some centuries later in the United States, termed 'Manifest Destiny' and in the British Empire's imperialistic ambitions; the same assumptions that, even now, export an industrialised economy to every corner of our Earth – that was, and is, so destructive, violent and ultimately nihilistic.

---

[22] Plutarch, *The Parallel Lives*, Vol. VII, Loeb Classical Library Edition. http://penelope.uchicago.edu/Thayer/E/Roman/Texts/Plutarch/Lives/Caesar*.html

[23] Hannah Osborne, 'Roman genocide: Battlefield where Julius Caesar slaughtered 150,000 tribespeople discovered in Netherlands', *International Business Times*, 12 December 2015. www.ibtimes.co.uk/roman-genocide-battlefield-where-julius-caesar-slaughtered-150000-tribespeople-discovered-1533067.

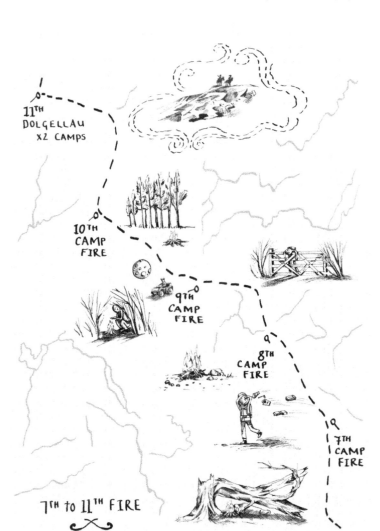

11TH
DOLGELLAU
x2 CAMPS

10TH
CAMP
FIRE

9TH
CAMP
FIRE

8TH
CAMP
FIRE

7TH
CAMP
FIRE

7TH to 11TH FIRE

Map 3

Day 6: Wednesday, 7 January

Knighton was special. In my mind it was a threshold. If I could claw my way to Knighton, I could stride to Mona. I decided to celebrate with a haircut, and it was an exquisitely good decision. As I reclined in a softly padded chair, the young woman made desultory enquiries as to my reasons for visiting her town. Responding to my reply, she astonished me by revealing that she was avidly reading about Stone-Age Britain. My own prejudice had assumed disinterest, and I felt both grateful and humbled by this animated, informed fellow traveller. The haircut took rather longer than planned as we swapped stories, questions and dreams. Just before I left, I told her about Manda Scott's *Boudica* novels and she wrote the information down. It was with a glad and uplifted heart that I pondered my options, as I turned to bring the sun onto my left shoulder and orientate northwest. I became aware of the proximity of Offa's Dyke, and with this information came two options: the more northerly and strenuous route, following the eighth-century Mercian king's rampart, still in large part delineating the border between Wales and England, or the valley that cut what I estimated to be a more direct route. A sober assessment of my physical condition and the arctic forecast my hairdresser friend had imparted tuned me to the latter. It was not an easy decision because I loved the idea of moving on to the hills and following the ancient earthwork, but the journey had instructively informed me of my limitations and I was obliged to comply.

The long valley-walk from Knighton to the distant ridge of hills yielded the most intense cold. Somewhere between −9 and −15°C in Wales at 1000-ft altitude was a unique and memorable experience for me. For the first and only time, I found and met a farmer who clearly owned the land upon which I wished to camp. It took some time for him to comprehend my request, but eventually, and with a shrug of his shoulders, he gave me the nod and I picked my way across the frigid ground to a fallen tree, where I thought to make my lair. With the cold seeping into every crevice, my water filter had become unusable, frozen, paralysed and inert. The combination of tiredness, lack of food, too little water and cold was slowing me down. I was extremely focused that evening as I tried to light my fire and thaw the filter, a small but critically important piece of equipment. Having found a dead sheep half-immersed in the river's shallows as I foraged for twigs to get my fire going, I was nervous of becoming unwell in such exposed and isolated circumstances. That night, I slept the way the sheep looked.

Day 7: Thursday, 8 January

Miles rolled and the following day I climbed to 1,600 ft before seeing Newtown below me, to the north. For the first time upon entering a town or village, I had a bad feeling in my gut. Hereford had been difficult, but that was mostly to do with my own state of mind. This felt different. I didn't recognise it as a premonition, but I believe it was, and some part of me also thought so. As I slowly descended to the town, on impulse I pulled the small voice recorder from my pocket and said,

'I feel like I'm entering hostile territory.'

Twenty minutes later, with traffic thronging the roads and shadows lengthening as the sun plunged below the horizon, I found myself on the verge of a main road, waiting to cross. Canting towards me was a red Ford Fiesta. As it drew close, the windows wound down and the car slowed. Anger, abuse and hate spewed from the contorted features of five young men as they jostled and competed for my attention. I was pelted with burgers, paper mugs, tin cans and what seemed like sacks of rubbish. The car made as if to stop and one of the doors swung open. In that moment, I knew that I was marked for attack. All kinds of unfamiliar sensations flooded my mind and body and for a few brief moments, I saw myself as they saw me: different, an outsider, friendless and set apart; incomprehensible, a victim, defenceless, an enemy and a rare opportunity. Unconsciously, perhaps, they had seen true. I *was* the man who had witnessed the outpouring of decaying junk food, offal disgorged from the indifferent inhabitants of a parallel world, and had cursed them. I *was* the critical commentator who judged their world and, truth be known, feared it. I *was*, and I *am*, the man who, too often, leaves insight and compassion strewn alongside the crud I name 'ugly'. A face contorted with animosity leered from the open car door, and I braced myself for what was to follow. I expected to be confronted, surrounded and then have a brief, noisy hiatus, before the first lunge and ensuing brawl. At the point of shrugging my pack to the ground, the car accelerated away and the traffic continued its indifferent trawl towards the traffic lights. Alert to the possibility that the car might be hosting a debate on the merits of finishing what they had started, I grabbed my pack and slipped into a side street, working my way southwest and searching for a place to stay the night. A stile, overgrown with brambles, gave me access to a track that looked rarely used and, following this, I made my way alongside a riverbank, checking footpaths as I probed for a place to conceal my camp. I felt uneasy that night and did not sleep well. The premonition of danger, the incident itself and the proximity of people all combined to keep me wary and tense. I felt depressed that I had, so quickly, succumbed to 'fight or flight'. In my immediate response to the antagonistic posturing of the youths, I saw the reflection of my own insecurity. I knew that, if a similar situation had occurred in my professional life, I would have probably found my way to less reactive and more creative options; yet, in this circumstance, I had assumed a blind alley and danced to the tune I had been thrown.

Day 8: Friday, 9 January

I was up early the following morning and threading my way back along the way I had come, as I looked for a passage over the river. Dark and unwarranted thoughts about this small town persisted, as I realised that I must have walked a loop of about five miles to make one in the direction I was intending. It was this, my aching body and the persistent dead weight of my pack that led me to a radical decision; I stopped by a layby just outside the town and abandoned my wheat flour to the hedgerow. It may not sound like much, but from my point of view I was emptying months of aspiration, planning, hard labour and applied research into that hedge, and it hurt. That I considered the disposal of one kilogram from my pack's overall weight as justification for this action suggests to me that I was either desperate or sinking into hopelessness. By late morning, I was following the river valley's northern side, somewhat cheered by the sun, but depleted, and close to sleeping even as I walked. Coming to a farm gate, I unceremoniously dumped my bag and then draped myself over the gate, in much the same way I used to dry a tent; I do believe I fell asleep.

'Are you okay?' the voice solicited, concerned, almost apprehensive. I came round with a jerk, unwrapping myself from the gate and trying to find the ground with my feet.

'Er, yes, just tired.' Appraising silence, but no judgement.

'Where've you come from?'

'The Malvern Hills.'

'No wonder you're tired.' Spotting an opportunity, I blurted my truth.

'Do you have any eggs?'

Rob had the look of a farmer's son, which is what he was. He was strong, young and reaching out into the world. He was also warm-hearted and curious. Like another couple I had met in Presteigne on my way to Knighton, Rob took me into his home and emptied the contents of his fridge onto the kitchen table. I was not there long, but his burgeoning hospitality and companionable manner was a salve on the harsh experiences of the last twenty-four hours. Within minutes of the kettle emitting its first hysterical shriek, we had established rapport and become interested in each other's story. He had returned to see his parents for a few days, and to recover after a series of late nights and uninhibited beer drinking. Rugby was his passion. He loved hunting, was politically conservative and preferred an almost exclusively carnivorous diet. I clearly inhabited a different and rather more complex, if also conspicuously less abundant, world. He thought that life was to be consumed in ever-larger mouthfuls, lubricated with alcohol and stabilised with values that emphasised family, common sense, honesty, integrity and hospitality. To all this, I had very little to contribute since, in a fug of blissful contentment and mild envy, it all made perfect sense to me. Rob had his delightful fiancée to meet, and I was late for my next karmic encounter. If we ever meet again, I will be delighted to see Rob. I had a sense of his courageous spirit, and the pathway of becoming towards which he was headed. Just before we parted company at the gate, he glanced at my pack and, clearly remembering the condition in which he had found me, asked if he could lift it, to gain a sense of its weight. Probably imagining that he would be greatly impressed at the stupefying weight with which I had burdened myself for this mythic journey, I nodded my assent. The result was shocking for us both. Rather like reaching to grasp an oak tree stump, he braced himself with legs bent and back straight, before lifting. The rucksack that had derided my manhood ever since I had first struggled up the lane at Embercombe abandoned Newton's law of universal gravitation and became obsequiously weightless. Rob's limbs flexed and extended, the backpack shot vertically upwards and we both stood startled and nonplussed, gazing at its bulky self-importance framed against the chill, blue sky. I've never felt quite the same about my backpack since this incident.

Navigating without a map or compass was important to me. I wished to be informed by the land itself, reading the signs, hazarding guesses and accepting the consequences. Maps are wonderful, but beyond their enticement is the stark truth that you are a latecomer, walking a trail that has been worn thin by those of your known world that have gone before. In older days, maps became more vague as they stretched from the familiar to the mythical. 'HC SVNT DRACONES' (here be dragons) adorns the 1510 Hunt-Lennox globe and, in its day, it could not have failed to entrance and terrify the armchair explorer. I wanted the intimacy of meeting my land anew. That I would inevitably be placing my feet in the imprints of bygone ancient kin no longer extant was not the same as explorers, many of whose names we still remember. I searched for a sense of belonging, of place, of inclusion; I searched for home. The implication of this was that I would inevitably find myself walking valleys dominated by roads that, largely indifferent to their aesthetic impact, transport the vast tonnage of our hearts' desires around the country. Like millions of others, I travel in my car admiring and appreciating the countryside from the warmth and purr of my car's snug interior, but, experienced from the roadside, it is very different. The verges of our main roads are dining tables along whose length carrion-feeders scavenge a good living. The disheartening swathe of rubbish endlessly garlands the green ribbon of land, buffering road from field, and the screams of mauled, crushed and broken animals rise and fall as lives tumble to the overwhelming force of our civilised world. The cold was intensifying again, as I meditated on the rhythmic tapping on my stick. I was beginning to think of my next camp when I came across a rabbit, its hips crushed with tiny shattered bones protruding through the soft fur of its beautiful little body. Eyes starting from its head and suffering terribly, it still tried to crawl away from me as I knelt to inspect its wounds. Suffering and pain are endemic to life, but there was something horrifying about the indifference of our cars and lorries to this small and gentle life, something so pathetic and lonely about this creature's life dribbling away on a frozen roadside. I was crying as I called a blessing to accompany the spirit of this rabbit, a blessing that rose and fell with each successive squadron of cars as they swept by, intent; worlds within worlds. Crying, I squared myself for the only compassionate task that felt within my power. Crying as I pounded the little body with my stick and drove the life from its fragile, impermanent niche. Some words of D.H. Lawrence kept repeating themselves in my mind as the tapping of my stick resumed and, each time, fresh tears welled and spilt.

'I never saw a wild thing sorry for itself.'

I did not know it at the time, but the valley that so conveniently sliced northwest from Pontdolgoch had already been commandeered by the A470. Even if I had found anyone to consult and explore alternatives, later study of maps showed me that I was boxed in, with no other realistic choices. In any case, I practised and eventually achieved some mastery in screening out the traffic that thundered, rumbled, whined and wheezed its way past me. My mind was elsewhere. With a Roman fort at Caersws, there is no doubt that patrols would have been sent up this Ordovices valley; no doubt that it would have been watched and monitored by eyes, well-hidden high above, on hilltops that retreated into the wild interior.

Darkness flowed across the land. With growing unease, I had to keep walking, as I was still moving through Carno, and there was nowhere I could identify as a potential hideaway. As dusk melted into night and, with the moon almost full, I saw my opportunity. Across a meadow glistening and sparkling, I saw what looked like an area of rough ground close to a railway track. For some reason, while the land felt welcoming, the human presence did not. I felt a cautionary disquiet and, like the hunting owl, stealth was my guide. I took a long time watching from the shadows of the hedge as I absorbed the pattern of fields, the angle of the moon and the options I had available to me. I could not see it, but I could hear the bellow of a tractor and the vaguest intimation of barn lights glowing sulphurous in the frozen, winter landscape some way to my left. With the decision made, and a sharp intake of breath, I climbed the gate and ran quickly to a hedge that I hoped would screen me if anyone happened to glance in my direction; my cover failed. Some way past the half-way mark, I thought I heard a shout, and shortly after that the cough of a quad bike spluttering into life. Already committed, I ran a further seventy-five yards and gratefully saw a small stretch of fence that I could straddle, before leaping over a small brook and clambering up the side of a steeply angled ditch. The quad bike was dashing across the field, coughing and spluttering as the engine complained against the cold start, and the rider dismounted to open a gate. Now, regaining my breath and feeling less exposed, I dropped down to the ground and knelt behind a screen of frost-encrusted reeds and tall grasses. I was on the run, thinking fast, weighing options and never letting my eyes drift from the headlights that were now methodically quartering the field and clearly searching for something. This was, perhaps, the coldest night of my journey. I was told in a nearby village that the temperature had plummeted to $-15°C$, and I hoped that this might work to my advantage. After sustaining his search mission over an impressively long period and coming very close to my lair, the headlights shifted back the way they had come, and I was left with a night so taut, brittle and whitely gleaming that I thought it might shatter, like the screen of some outsized drive-in movie screen. I don't know what the farmer saw that prompted his search, but something had alerted him. I felt his suspicion linger in the faint odour of the quad bike's exhaust, as it hung in the motionless air — aimless, unrequited and baleful.

Choosing my campsite before dark was important, since gathering wood by torchlight was a lot more hazardous and time-consuming. This time, I had no alternative but to work without either daylight or torchlight, but the moon came to help and, gradually, I began to feel more securely hidden. I had kindled a small fire behind a screen of woven bracken and twigs, and I nursed it assiduously as the entrancement of fire and sky began to seep inside my tired and aching limbs. There was no night more beautiful than this one. I had all my clothes on and for the first time had unwrapped the gleaming silver survival blanket, encasing myself in its wrinkled folds. My head reclined on a bed of moss, wedged under the bivi-bag only inches from the fire, and my eyes feasted on the hallowed grace of distant worlds.

Day 9: Saturday, 10 January

I was up early, and was well on my way by dawn. My experience in Newtown, the rabbit, the A470 trail of death, the extreme cold, eating and drinking too little and pushing myself hard were all taking their toll. That night I found refuge in a small conifer wood. The trees shut out the moon and, inexplicably, I found myself experiencing a sense of profound loneliness. I cannot remember admitting such a desolate sense of isolation and loss. Huddled on the steep hillside with a relentlessly cold breeze sweeping downhill among the gaunt tree stems, I floundered with feelings and emotions that belonged to another, younger era; I did not sleep more than an hour or so that night. The fire was my only protection and I felt flayed by the wild dogs of subconscious fears, doubts and past mistakes. It was almost a relief to be counting the Ribena, Lucozade and Red Bull cans once more when, driven from the hillside by my own dark introspection, I took to the road again, swinging my stick to the tempo of a song I was once taught in other times of trial and challenge.

Day 10: Sunday, 11 January

It was the swing and twist of my stick that eventually disarmed the tension and fear of the night before. The chaotic swirl of darkened shadows was translated into insights that preoccupied me for some months to come. I have always thought of myself as independent, happy with my own company and self-reliant, and, to a degree, I am. However, I have often confused my determination and capacity for single-minded pursuit of a goal or vision, whatever the consequences or costs, with a preference for solitude. Aloneness has been some part of the price exacted for following unusual pathways. The love and veneration for nature that I have experienced since a child is real, but I have also hidden behind it, as a defence against the more dangerous peril of risking a deep relationship with another, especially a woman.

Crouched on the hillside, I met the lie that I had held close to defend against hurt and pain. There was, within me, a deep longing for a love that I had studiously avoided for many years; a love not designed to fit within some lofty dream; an appendage that would complete a picture that existed somewhere in my imagination; a safely constructed dream figure who would play her part and read her lines. I felt shame at how I had treated those few who had penetrated my reality-screening, offered me the unconditional, unexalted love of home and hearth and who had been brushed aside by my fear of vulnerability. I felt shame, but I also felt compassion for the young and sensitive child within me, who knew no other way to protect himself and live some semblance of a powerful, directed and purposeful life.

61 CE, the Great Hall, Iceni Territory, the fenlands, East Britain

The Boudica, wife of the deceased Iceni chieftain Prasutagus, has witnessed the 'gang rape' of her daughters, and been publicly flogged by Roman troops acting on the orders of the Procurator, Decianus Catus, to teach her and the Iceni a lesson. A druid healer brushes the curtain of her lodge aside and walks out into the bright sunlight. She strides towards a small group of Iceni warriors who wait expectantly in the shade of a small copse of Ash trees.

'The augury is clear. Destiny dances in our eyes, painted in the colours of life or death. Even as we speak, the sacred isle, Mona, watches as the Beast (Suetonious Paulinius) prepares to leap. The Boudica will walk from her lodge when the sun rises tomorrow, and then we ride.'

From the outside edge of the circle a tall, lean man speaks. 'Where, Dark Shield, where do we ride?'

'We ride to Camulodunum.' She pauses, looking into the eyes of each man and woman. 'Then Londinium.' Her voice quietens, 'then Verulamium.' Slowly, with awful precision, 'and then, *every* village, town, garrison, staging post or battlefield, until we have driven these cursed people from our land forever.'

'Will the other tribes join us? We cannot do this thing alone!'

Dark Shield glances back towards the lodge where a chieftain is lain, as the strips of torn and shredded flesh are cut from her bloodied body and wounds cleaned. She sees past the lodge walls to the silent form of her friend, the prone woman whose outstretched arm reaches for the huddled, broken, desolated children she failed to protect.

'With or without the other tribes, we will ride into this wind, for who are we without our courage, our ceremonies, our willingness to stand? Perhaps, perhaps, raising our standard once more will pull the beast's legions from Mona in time, Red Hawk. For without Mona, we are a people exiled from our own soul-being, adrift, lost to the dreaming that guides us. Prepare, and be ready.'

In the week before I left Embercombe to begin my long walk, I received a visitor. Mike Gardner, a woodsman and much more besides, brought me a gift to assist my walk. It was a hazel stem that had been embraced by honeysuckle, as it had glided upwards towards the sun from beneath the high canopy of a nearby wood. In the constricting fragrant embrace of this native species, it had produced a spectacular sculpted spiral that curved sun-wise towards a cleft, where it branched and became two. It was a slim, magician's wand, a companion, a crutch and a staff to assist my passage across steep ground, or patches of ice. I trimmed it to size and embarked on an intensely personal and intimate relationship with this stick, as we walked the whole journey together. Quite early on, it assumed a precocious, prickly, know-it-all attitude that had us rapt in contentious debate – petulant and disagreeable. On occasion, I had to assert control and place an order of silence on it. This usually led to periods of scarcely disguised resentment with snide, recriminatory comments and disobliging twists as it struck the ground. Most of these incidents flared up over the stick's name. Self-important by inclination, it wanted a name that conferred some dignity and authority. I, on the other hand, frequently feeling that I was doing most of the journey's domestic and less-glamorous duties, believed that a name of such stature should be earned. At the risk of unfairly using the advantage of being the author of these words, I should also state that I was both impressed and deeply appreciative of the burden I impressed upon my stick, when bending under the apathetic weight of my backpack. 'Drum' was a name that was favoured by both of us for a while as worthy and honourable, until the stick felt it contained an undertone of monotony, and it was abandoned. Things really came to a head when, after a particularly gruelling schlep along the remaining section of the A470, the stick suddenly announced that it wished to be called 'Gaia'. This is the name that William Golding suggested to the British scientist James Lovelock when he developed the hypothesis of the Earth as a self-regulating system: the Gaia Hypothesis. Gaia was a Greek goddess, the mother of all; she was the Earth.

I raised an objection on the basis that this was a gross and grandiose inflation of the stick's true nature; that then led to an extremely difficult, and occasionally acrimonious, dialogue about self-worth, value and identity. Neither of us earned any commendations for this interchange, and things did not look too good until we finally found its true and authentic name. We were shocked into silence when, from the maelstrom of accusation, denial and blame-shifting, the name of Gaia was spoken with a soft 'g' and became irrevocably changed. From this, like a phoenix rising from the ashes of our inflamed relationship, emerged... Gyre: 'A circular movement in which each circle is above, below or wider than the one before', declares the Cambridge Dictionary website.[24]

---

[24] 'Gyre', Cambridge Dictionary. https://dictionary.cambridge.org/dictionary/english/gyre.

My staff ('stick' had now been cast aside as an inadequate, even demeaning term, and substituted) approved and, for the next day or so, would declaim Yeats' famous lines from his poem, 'The Second Coming'.

> Turning and turning in the widening gyre
> The falcon cannot hear the falconer;
> Things fall apart; the centre cannot hold;
> Mere anarchy is loosed upon the world...[25]

From that time on, Gyre and I became unified in our endeavour, and joined by a similarly dark, yet uplifting, vision of our shared undertaking, we picked up the pace and veered north for the giant's chair, Cader Idris. It is said that anyone who sleeps on the lower slopes of this legendary Welsh mountain risks awakening insane. Contemplating what, even to us, was an odd and disquieting interlude, Gyre and I made efforts to circumnavigate the mountain in one big push. It was on this day, 11 January, that the weather began to break. Forging our way up the mountain pass, the wind howled and shrieked, buffeting my already-weary body and provoking a resurgent outpouring of joy. It was as if the ice within me had melted as, with bellowing discharge, huge ice blocks tumbled into the canyon of all past endeavour. It was not long before rain came sweeping in from the southwest. A drenching, freezing, invasive, penetrating rain that pried the crevices of my dishevelled person, and chilled me as the extreme cold had not. By the time I trudged into Dolgellau, it was pitch black; I was limping and very cold. The whole town seemed deserted – a kind of forlorn, civic *Mary Celeste*. It seemed to me that I should rest and not be too conflicted about finding a safe haven where I could recover my strength, before striking out again. Spiritually, I was in a state of grace; physically, I was depleted. Banging on the doors of a house that sported the minimalist message 'Bed & Breakfast' and hearing only the

---

[25] W.B. Yeats, 'The Second Coming', *The Collected Poems of W.B. Yeats* (1989).

sound of my echoing fist, I approached a couple of locals who were standing outside a pub entrance, braving the weather to tug on a cigarette. They were gratifyingly helpful and waved me on down the street where I found refuge. The sleep I enjoyed that night felt like a death. I lay upon the bed and the lights went out.

Day 11: Monday, 12 January

The following morning, Dolgellau looked very different. The atmosphere of grim foreboding had dissipated, and in its place was a delightful, bustling, friendly small town. I luxuriated in the warm cosiness of a small café, ate cakes and lounged in a local hotel with a newspaper. The contrast with the world with which I had become familiar over the last ten days was bewildering, but my body was grateful, and I resolved to stay another night before leaving the next day. Something I ate that day, however, poisoned my system and before too long I was intermittently crouched on the bathroom floor, vomiting into the toilet bowl or clawing myself onto my feet and sitting on it. Either way, the experience was overwhelmingly unpleasant and what little strength I had garnered from the previous night's sleep was soon dissipated. Bathed in sweat, running a temperature and even after several hours' uncontrollable retching, I was at least thankful that I was alone and unobserved. The B&B proprietor was showing some signs of discomfiture at the odd behaviour of her new guest as the toilet chain, like a ship's watch, gloomily tolled the passing of time. No sign of life was registered from Room 3 until mid-morning the following day, when I emerged, gaunt, wan and somewhat diminished. I made my way shakily down the stairs, thanked a rather circumspect host, and wobbled falteringly out into the morning sun.

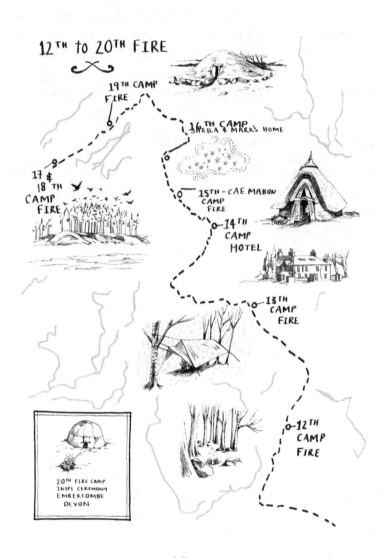

12TH to 20TH FIRE

19TH CAMP FIRE

16TH CAMP
STELLA & MARK'S HOME

17 & 18TH CAMP FIRE

15TH – CAE MABON CAMP FIRE

14TH CAMP HOTEL

13TH CAMP FIRE

12TH CAMP FIRE

20TH FIRE CAMP
INIPI CEREMONY
EMBERCOMBE
DEVON

Map 4

Day 12: Tuesday, 13 January

Finding my way across the river, I slipped out of Dolgellau immensely relieved to be feeling almost normal, and thankful for the peace and solitude of the unwinding trail. I was entering the southernmost edge of territory with which I had once been familiar. My time living in North Wales had been seminal in my spiritual development. It was by the sea and in the mountains of this land that I had heard the elders speak; in the familiar scents of rock, moss, tree and stream I could feel the whispering of the ancient ones. Silken threads of memory, the music of dialects left to echo against the granite cliffs, the sense of water permeating every hollow, always moving, probing and seeking the ocean. Not for the first time, I felt myself walking on the edge of another parallel world – only this time I was going in. Making my way between two large rock outcrops perched high above on the shoulders of Maes Mawr, I fancied I saw a rider turn his horse about and, glancing down towards me, call out to a companion not yet in view. Silhouetted on the hilltop, he looked proud and vital, a shield strapped to the horse's flank and a sheathed sword slung diagonally across his back. I blinked, involuntarily calling out words in a language I have never learned, the prickle of hairs rising on my neck. Energy pulsed as my body responded, breath quickening; an elated surge of recognition. Gatekeepers of the high mountain fastness, they drifted in and out of focus while, all the time, my heart leapt the gap that separated us and strove to hold the ephemeral close. Arms outstretched skyward, I threw my voice upward, uncaring of passers-by, intent only upon walking the bridge between. The images fluctuated, dispelled and coalesced, once more firm and momentarily substantial. The rider was joined by a companion whose hair swept the sky dark and for a few moments more they saluted my arrival, as the horses impatiently awaited the deft touch to signal time to run again. I sat down by a small stream and, filling my flask, drank the mountain water. I had many more miles to go, but any doubt of not making it to Mona had dispersed in the mist of horse breath, which now shrouded the hill of my erstwhile comrades.

I was glad to see the forest ahead, glad to know that it would fold a robe around my shoulders and hold me close. Alongside the Iceni chariot ring, the purpose of my dream pathway was heavy in my pocket. The sheer effort of shifting the gears of my body as I set one foot in front of the other, and the subtle, demanding pull of the felt, yet scarcely visible, imaginal world was taking its toll. Along with the debilitating impact of my 'rest' in Dolgellau, I was aware that it was time to pause and attentively listen. Knowing that I was walking in a roughly northerly direction, I chose to await invitation and follow wherever my belly-heart took me. Of all the paths I might have taken, the one I chose took me to an oak tree upon which was pinned a very carefully decorated letter. At the foot of the tree was a small ceramic vase with the bleached remains of some flowers. As I read the words and felt into the woman that had written them, I was very moved. There is such dignity and beauty in our small lives and the tenderness of our coming and going. I include the text of this message here, so that the love expressed in this small hand-written note can continue to swim from heart to heart and sing the story of these people – people I have never met, but whose lives touched mine:

> Greg, what can I say, mate? What can any of us say? Only that we are all going to miss you so much. I'll never forget the time we all spent together. We had some really good days and laughs. Your cheeky smile will stay in my thoughts always. Thanks for being there for me when I needed a shoulder to cry on. And I don't think I got the chance to say how grateful I am. Until we meet again I will see you in my dreams and keep you safe in my heart. Rest in peace my love. Love as always,
>
> Louise, Jay and the boys

Even in the freezing midwinter, the soft, richly perfumed forest floor was ornamented with lichens and mosses, ferns and tall grasses. I took my time, marvelling at this woodland equivalent of a coral reef. Life erupting in cascades of green luminescence, flowing over tumbled rocks; a lattice of tiny caves and hidden recesses that gave entry to the dark, dreaming world of dryads, and banished pagan deities who, like bandits, still found refuge in the miniature ravines of liminal worlds. Somewhere deep inside Coed y Brenin Forest Park I came to a standstill and, easing my way through the thick undergrowth at the trail's edge, I entered into the sterile gloom of the coniferous plantation's underbelly. It was a good place to build my shelter with plenty of dry, dead wood, but something that had been gnawing at my awareness began to thrust itself forward – assertive, demanding attention. It was not so much the depressing human-industrial aesthetic that these conifer plantations smear on the uplands they have invaded, or indeed the relatively impoverished ecological habitats they provide. It was the realisation that, across the many miles of upland country that I had tramped this last couple of weeks, forest of any kind had been conspicuously absent. Over the last five years I have become increasingly aware of the 'rewilding' movement,[26] and George Monbiot's book *Feral*[27] brought many disparate threads together in my mind. However, it was in undertaking the task of writing this book, when I pored over maps, listened to my recorded voice and revisited Wales in my car, that I saw our land as she is. 'Broken' is a word Alan Watson Featherstone, of Trees for Life, uses, and that is how it feels to me. With only 13% tree cover,[28] the UK is one of the least-wooded areas in Europe (37% for the European Union), and only a third of this paltry 13% is given over to native woodland.

---

[26] www.rewildingbritain.org.uk.

[27] George Monbiot, *Feral* (London, Penguin, 2014).

[28] Forestry Commission, 2011 and Forestry Commission, 2010. www.forestresearch.gov.uk/tools-and-resources/statistics/statistics-by-topic/woodland-statistics/.

George Monbiot commented in a recent talk I attended at Exeter University that, if when travelling through Europe you look up to the mountains, you see forest. Do the same in Britain and you see a bare, 'sheep-wrecked'[29] and denuded landscape. Naked hillsides, the undressed curves of a body shorn, relentlessly controlled, deprived of self-will and the capacity to nurture abundance.

Broken can be mended. The rewilding movement is not the simplistic, naive fantasy that its critics would seek to portray it as. It is one of those collectively acquired, rare, graced insights, which allows old assumptions to acquiesce and concede to a deeper truth. In due course it will wipe away the scales from our eyes and facilitate the emergence of a deeper wisdom. It will take us one step closer to perceiving nature as she really is: an infinitely well-designed architecture of interdependent, interrelated and interconnected fronds, which intelligently and joyously howl the anthem that we call life. Our hubris, whether expressed in the benevolence of kindly patrician values that unconsciously control, while assuming motives supporting the common good, or the uninhibited megalomania of a consumerist society that justifies any action as worth the price, is the burden that the Titan, Atlas, really carries.

Rewilding Britain is the charity set up to reverse the landslide of ecological harm that we have, mostly unwittingly and often uncaringly, visited upon our home. Their mini-manifesto states their aims – to:

o   reverse the loss of biodiversity in large core areas of land and sea
o   reintroduce key missing species, including the lynx and wolf
o   restore ecosystems to a functional and resilient state
o   reignite people's passion for the natural world
o   revitalise local economies in ways that work ecologically
o   reintegrate nature and society for the benefit of both

---

[29] George Monbiot's term.

At the centre of the rewilding movement is the hope of a better future. Walking the land of our tribal ancestors, passing the abandoned remains of ceremonial sites where we once gathered to express our awe and reaffirm our kinship with the natural world, it came to me that we live inside a story of shame. We dare not declare it because we would then have to do something about it and, in any case, the humiliation is too terrifying to contemplate. We have betrayed the covenant that is the Children's Fire, and shame is the crippling cost of this fall from grace; shame is the gulf that stands as a void between who we could be, and who we have become. The rewilding of our land would be an active and courageous admission of our youthful culpability as a society, a pledge to future generations, and would enable a spiritual renewal that would sweep away the morbid haunting of our species' end-of-term school report: 'Could do better'. What is embedded inside the rewilding concept is a dynamic call to action, an opportunity to redeem the vision of a peaceful, just and truly beautiful world.

***

In a shelter constructed of fallen branches, a tree stump and heaped pine needles, I fashioned a home for the night and gave myself to sleep. I then arose, weightless, to drink at the well of dreams and stand upon the far shore, waiting for a tryst with those who have blessed me with these turbulent years of fierce becoming.

> ONCE in the dream of a night I stood
> Lone in the light of a magical wood,
> Soul-deep in visions that poppy-like sprang;
> And spirits of Truth were the birds that sang,
> And spirits of Love were the stars that glowed,
> And spirits of Peace were the streams that flowed
> In that magical wood in the land of sleep.
>
> Lone in the light of that magical grove,
> I felt the stars of the spirits of Love

Gather and gleam round my delicate youth,
And I heard the song of the spirits of Truth;
To quench my longing I bent me low
By the streams of the spirits of Peace that flow
In that magical wood in the land of sleep.

Song of a Dream, Sarojini Naidu

62 CE, the deep forest, Ordovician territory, a few months after Boudica's last great battle and defeat

A small band of Iceni warriors travel under cover of darkness towards Mona. Many suffer disfigurements and scarcely healed wounds from an encounter with a Roman patrol. A young girl sleeps fitfully in the arms of her uncle, as he fords the chill waters of a stream. Ahead, one of the scouts snakes towards them like a returning shadow. She motions for silence.

'Ahead, one hundred paces, in the hazel grove by the mountain shoulder. They rest, but their guards are alert.'

'They would be,' growls the Boar Clan warrior bringing up the rear, 'they wouldn't see another dawn if the centurions caught them sleeping on guard duty.'

The man carrying the girl sets her down softly, his eyes signalling danger, commanding her silence. His gaze moves across the weary, pained-etched faces of comrades dedicated to the moon's teachings, now held in the rhymed memory of a young child – the last one living. Clasping his brother's arm, an older man speaks.

'Fox, we understand. We always have. The Gliding One will take us forward. When you hear the alarm raised, take the young dreamer and press through to the west. There is still time before the ship leaves Mona.'

A pause deep enough to drown in; a quiet that insinuates the night, as frost steals on blades of brittle grass; friends who will never meet again.

'Forever welcome at my hearth. Forever close to my heart.'

The man's powerful arms reach out and the girl steps forward as he hefts her onto his back. The shadow slips into the darkness again and the men follow. Fox waits. A challenge, a call to arms. The dark night explodes into chaos. The man's breath comes in short snatches, as he works his way through the dead stems of last year's bracken. He prays to the mountain goddess as the girl child clutches at his cloak and presses her face into the musky warmth of his neck. In spite of everything, she feels safe. Nothing can harm her warrior uncle. Meanwhile, a few hundred paces behind, lives are lost and hope bleeds into the dark earth.

Day 13: Wednesday, 14 January

As I emerged from the forest on Wednesday 14 January, I began to realise that I must have inadvertently veered northeast along a tributary of the Afon Eden, thinking that I was still following the main river. I felt both nourished and disorientated by the forest, interested in how the enclosed, secretive mystery of the trees had intensified an introspective reverie, and limited my capacity for perspective, larger patterns and proportion. As I probed the valleys, seeking higher ground and sensing a change in the weather, I found myself musing on how landscapes sculpt and form the mindset and culture of the people living within them, and how we, in turn, impose our ideas and beliefs on the environment. My reverie was cut short as clouds came scudding in from the southwest. I crested another hill and settled into the day's walking, with Gyre reaching out before me like the pendulum of an old clock.

Trawsfynydd nuclear power station eventually loomed on the far horizon. Even from a distance it looked massive, alien and somehow malefic. A grey shroud of bleak loneliness seemed to hang, suspended in the hemisphere of winter sky that wrapped its long, thin arms around the huge concrete silo. I passed an isolated smallholding and, as I paused to drink some water, saw a lone figure working with a mattock, clearing a ditch. She looked beautiful. Flinging the mattock above her head with arms extended, she was systematically working the length of the ditch, hauling mud and weed onto the bank. A quality of vigour, wholeheartedness and self-sufficiency radiated from every gesture. Sure-footed and purposeful, she worked with focused intention, scarcely pausing to sweep a thick, exuberant pelt of grey hair back over her shoulder. There was something about this woman that was intensely familiar, significant and compelling. Within the space of time it takes a struck match to flare, I saw us exchange a few words, link hands, walk to her home and, on rugs before a blazing open fire, collide in an ecstasy of moist heat, entwined limbs and the swollen surge of winter tides curling, spiralling and heaping upon the soft contours of a secluded beach. Stepping forward, I took a breath and tilted my head back to call but, even as the sound grew in my throat, I had the distinct feeling that she would prefer to be left undisturbed. Reeling from the vivid intensity of my daydream, confused and disconcerted, I drew back. The figure in the field continued to dance and swerve along the ditch, occasionally leaping the water, and seemingly oblivious of the bedraggled, unkempt tramp that peered in her direction from beyond the fence. The worn blade of the mattock caught threads of grey light and reflected them back to the soft dark earth, as the apparition continued her work and I shifted to a more mundane reality. Abruptly, Gyre swung forward, taking the lead to avoid further embarrassment. Within a few seconds my stride was lengthening, as I recovered my poise sufficiently to enjoy a further brief glimpse into one possible – albeit forsaken – future.

Fifteen miles later, and once again very tired, I arrived on a hill above Ffestiniog, knowing that the following day I would reach Beddgelert and the familiar haunts of a previous life-chapter. All along the trail, I had passed among traces of Rome's military and economic preoccupations. Kilns for the firing of tiles, the Sarn Helen trail reaching up from South Wales and Tomen y

Mur fort all shout the story of Agricola's tenure as governor of Britain, and his campaign against the Ordovices. Tacitus records that, after inflicting a bloody defeat on a Roman cavalry unit, the Ordovices tribe were almost entirely wiped out in 78 CE, as Agricola made reprisals and strove to effect a permanent solution. It is moments of history like this that I still find myself incapable of fully absorbing. Is there any species on Earth more given to killing than us? Whatever numinous qualities we possess – and they are many – it is impossible to avoid noticing our predilection for violence and premeditated cruelty. In his disturbing, exciting and thought-provoking book *Sapiens*, Yuval Noah Harari[30] comments on the plasticity of our minds when young, asserting that, in comparison to most other mammals, we are born in a premature condition and suggestible to whatever influences, whether benign or malign, that may be brought to bear.

It is the malleability of our developing personality that gives such scope and dimension to our potential for learning. It is the very same quality that makes us so susceptible to experiences that result in learning that is anti-social, fearful, and very deeply embedded. What is amusing in the child, often engendering an indulgent response, may well become dangerous in the adult as he, or she, gradually develops agency in the world. In the soft tissue of the young mind, trauma fixates and teaches attitudes, assumptions and behaviours that we later condemn and punish. The unconscious acceptance of an essentially sociopathic society that flies in the face of the Children's Fire may have diverse roots in our species' history, but one of them is evident in the freedoms that were torn from the tribal people of this land two millennia ago.

I set up my shelter on the uplands, looking down to Ffestiniog, as the rain and wind arrived, crawling into my sleeping bag wet and chilled. I slept for fourteen hours that night.

---

[30] Yuval Noah Harari, *Sapiens* (London, Harvill Secker, 2014).

Day 14: Thursday, 15 January

The following day I walked another twenty miles, eventually arriving in Beddgelert shortly before dark. My Achilles tendons were hurting and swollen, my back and hips pulsated with pain and the weather was turning from bad to worse. With battered pride, I was coming to a slow, grudging and mostly erratic acceptance that I really was profoundly tired and in need of a place to recuperate. It is seven-and-a-half miles from Beddgelert to Pen-y-Gwryd Hotel, and over that distance the land rises nearly 800 feet. Never having fully expunged the images of a demented and anguished King Lear, lunging at me from the television screen of my kindly host outside Hereford, I was unwillingly dragged back into a world of utter darkness, howling wind and drenching rain. My pack joined forces with Gyre and against my best intentions I was persuaded to call a taxi.

'Hello?'

'Hello, can I book a taxi please?'

'Yes, of course my dear, what's your name?'

'Mac.'

'So where are you, Mac, and where do you want to go to?'

'I'm outside the Tanronnen Inn in Beddgelert and I wondered if you could take my backpack to the Pen-y-Gwryd Hotel?'

There was a pause as my request was considered before the warm, compassionate voice continued. 'And is your backpack with you, Mac?'

'Yes, it's been with me the whole way.'

'The whole way is it, I see, but you personally don't want to go to the Pen-y-Gwryd Hotel?'

'Oh no, I do; but I need to walk.'

'You need to walk, do you?'

Quietly, almost inaudibly: 'Yes.' Then silence as Gyre, the backpack and me struggle to retain some semblance of composure.

'Well now, you see, it's like this, Mac. I can take your backpack, but it will cost no more if you were to keep it company, it being such a horrendous night and all that.'

'Thank you, yes, I understand, but I really do need to walk. It's very tempting but...'

Patiently, and speaking to me as a mother would to a child, 'Look see, Mac, is it a secret? The thing is no one except me and you will know, and I'm not for telling anybody...'

A dark portentous silence, and my first felt experience of dark matter. 'Alright Mac, I'll be right over and if you want to change your mind just jump in as well.'

My taxi driver was a very kind and wonderful woman. She clearly did not understand why I was so determined to walk and did everything in her power to help me make a more sensible decision. The storm was now taking on epic proportions, and the light of the village was abruptly truncated just a few paces beyond the pub. Obsidian darkness wrapped itself around the land of the living, and everything sounded of water. We loaded the pack into the boot of her car and I paid her, before watching as the rear lights bleated their pathetic farewell, and the car was swallowed into the dark maw of night. Three times that evening my taxi-driving friend happened to pass me, and each time she wound the taxi window down to check if I was okay. She repeatedly offered to take me up the long valley at no extra charge, and in response to my refusal, never failed to offer me the chance to change my mind.

Close enough to touch but invisible in the gullet of the storm hunched Dinas Emrys. Girdled by story, myth and song, this small hill is one of the rumoured sites for Caratacus' last stand. Entirely focused on putting one foot in front of another, I flinched from the bony fists of numberless ghosts reaching out and clawing at my resolve. The shouts of warriors surging to stem a break in the line, the screaming of the maimed horses and humans, the killing lust of men getting down to business, the dread acknowledgement of imminent defeat, the eye of the storm and an opportunity to break free. What was in the mind of Caratacus as he escaped the melee and sought refuge with Cartimandua of the Brigantes? What then when the warm welcoming embrace of safe refuge dissolved in the duplicitous manoeuvring of friend-turned-foe? That night I was flayed by the livid memory of Caratacus' defeat and the vacuum into which spilled the fragile dreams of the many whose only hope lay curled within the fable of his invincibility.

Nothing can describe how I felt when, some hours later, moving painfully slowly through the deluge of rain that was sweeping like a curtain before me, I saw the lantern in the far distance. I staggered through the hotel doors, as many have before me, and slumped on to the reception desk.

'Are you the man who had his rucksack transported up the valley from Beddgelert?'

'Yes.'

'The taxi driver left this for you.'

I opened the proffered envelope and inside was half the fare that I had paid to her, along with a note suggesting that I might like to enjoy a drink with it. I was undone; the final straw. If I had been writing my will that evening, I would have left her everything.

I had missed dinner, but I did not care. I was incapable of thinking beyond the next step and, that evening, the next step was a bath. This wonderful, idiosyncratic throwback of a hotel had a bathroom to die for. It was an original Victorian bathroom with all kinds of pipes, taps, levers and tanks, and the bath was deep. That night, I experienced bliss; a hot bath may not be considered as usually invoking the highest plane of human consciousness, but it transported me to a place that I could easily claim to be heaven on Earth. Gallons of steaming-hot water, a body riven with aches and pains, no demand to meet anyone else's needs and a soft bed to follow. Murmuring gratitude to the gods and goddesses of Victorian invention, I lapsed into a parallel world and stayed there for as long as I could.

Day 15: Friday, 16 January

The following day was a cornucopia of comfort, pleasure and sensuous delight. I shifted from one alluring experience to the next, luxuriating in each and then, with stiff joints and the slow, careful adjustment of unco-operative limbs, fumbled to the next. This did not involve steam baths, fragrant oils, hot towels and the expert ministrations of softly voiced women. It did not involve the gentle massaging of my body with herbal compounds infused with the nectar of a thousand oriental flowers. Instead, and rather more prosaically, it entailed collapsing into well-worn armchairs and drinking tea in a cup and saucer; finding a window seat where the sun could caress my sleeping face and saying 'yes' to dessert, while asking for more gravy. It included embracing my friend, Tracker (who, the following day, was to walk with me down the Llanberis pass), and the easy comfort of a friendship that had endured many twists and turns. For one complete day, I knelt in wordless submission to the hotel's uncompromising and profoundly satisfying attitude towards life, hospitality and punctuality. Often lapsing into prolonged periods of time entirely devoid of thought or feeling, the hotel gong would summon me from the underworld and, like Orpheus, I would walk towards the upper world. Unlike Orpheus, however, I would steadfastly make my way towards the next meal, never looking back and, on that day at least, be firmly committed to living in the present. On one occasion, I ventured outside, only to find that yesterday's abyss of shrieking elemental powers had given way to soft, golden sunlight, innocent blue skies and the gentle cadence of a life at peace with itself.

I did not know it at the time, but I had slept just inside the perimeter of a 9.5-acre Roman marching camp. Sited as it was at the intersection of three mountain valleys in the heart of Ordovician territory, this camp was strategically crucial. Intermittently occupied by legionaries and auxiliary troops perhaps numbering around 3000, it can hardly have been a favourite location for the soldiers. Overlooked from above, and frequently subject to weather that would have allowed an implacable enemy to get disconcertingly close, undetected, I imagined the soldiers' relief as they woke to the steel grey of each successive dawn.

Day 16: Saturday, 17 January

That second night at Pen-y-Gwyrd Hotel, I had many dreams. Prior to the first successful ascent of Mount Everest, Sir Edmund Hillary and Tenzing Norgay were based here as they trained for their Himalayan expedition. Many other legendary names from the world of mountaineering, including John Hunt, Joe Brown, Noel Odell and Chris Bonnington, have also stayed at the hotel; behind them countless others, including the Romans and auxiliaries who first built the fort ramparts. Standing behind them: perhaps Ordovices tribespeople, possibly Gangani and Deceangli and, almost inevitably, druids from Mona. Wolves, bears, lynx, eagles, wandering bands of Neanderthals; so many layers of human, and more-than-human, history composted on this one, tiny patch of land.

Sunrise came at 7:57am that morning. With each passing day, the hours of light stretched longer as the Earth, tilted at an angle of 23.5°, wheeled around the sun and showed its northern face to the great light-bringer.

After I had completed my last hotel breakfast I strolled outside to study the weather. The early morning sunlight washed against the flanks of Eryri, a huge, golden torc curving on the mountain and announcing the soul of these wild hills to all those who seek to find their way home. Over a period of about twenty-five years, Tracker and I shared many very profound and sometimes extremely challenging experiences as we negotiated our lives and tried to find the right balance between the sacred and the profane. In my case, at least, this resembled a car that had approached a corner too fast, and having lost control, was steered by someone who consistently over-corrected, as they spun the wheel from one side to another. It made for an exciting, unstable and curiously predictable life. Along with several other close friends, Tracker had remained living in North Wales and it felt wonderful to be greeted by him that morning. Deep in conversation and revelling in the blessing of a sapphire sky, we descended the pass before parting company at Llanberis. We were not together for long, but there was significance in sharing this iconic trail, and passing into and between so many reminders of places, people and experiences that had brought us kneeling before the same altar. One of several parallel, deeply incised glacial valleys, the pass looks northwest to Mona, a ceremonial gateway guarding a last stand. When I had stood at the summit of the British Camp on the Malvern Hills more than two weeks previously and looked northwest, my gaze would have swept up to the highlands of Pen-y-Pass, paused in awe at these tombstone mountains and then stooped to the low-lying plain of an island, once called holy.

Chapter 4
The Netherworld

MY FIRST HOME in North Wales was a small cottage called Cae Goronwy, and was located in Fachwen, looking out over Llyn Padarn to the line of peaks that travel southeast to Snowdon. It was a picturesque location and, even then, almost unique for its inaccessibility. In January 1978 there was plenty of snow and, newly released from a full-time job, it fulfilled all of my criteria for a new beginning. Bob and Barbara Parry managed this gem for an owner who lived overseas, and for a tiny pittance they rented it to me. There was no heating, except for an open fireplace that nestled messily in a soot-blackened stone inglenook. Water was hand-pumped from a well, and the whole place smelt of wood, moss, stone and friendship. I gathered fuel from the nearby woods and washed my clothes in the stream; I bathed in the old magic of these great dreamer mountains and, unbeknown to me, made preparation for my life ahead. Together with other friends, we had arrived in the mountains over a short period of years, all set on carving a bid for freedom. In our late twenties, or very early thirties, and variously intoxicated with each other's bodies, the sea, wood smoke, the mountains, music, cannabis and psilocybin mushrooms, we were insatiate, devouring the wonder of being young, strong and having limitless energy. The winter was cold, and Cae Goronwy was impossible to heat properly, so I used to huddle close to the fire, inspired by, and contented with, my surroundings, even if my love life was a continuing drama of peaks and troughs. Maintaining enough wood for my fire was a challenge. After the first two months I was having to forage further and further afield looking for dead wood, and most days were taken up with the simple yet time-consuming process of domestic chores. Close by the cottage was a small copse of young silver birch trees; they were singularly beautiful. One afternoon, equipped with axe and saw, I capitulated to a desire to fell one of these trees. A confused mixture of irritation at the inconvenient distance I was required to carry my harvested timber, and my desire to wield my axe 'properly', led to a hurried, thoughtless and self-serving decision. The satisfaction was very brief and was quickly overwhelmed by the immediate knowledge that I had committed an act of sacrilege. I kept shoving the feeling down, trying to maintain a bluff, matter-of-fact, unsentimental attitude, but it was toppled by the inescapable knowledge that I had broken a pact. I had felled live trees before and I have done so since, but before this point I had never done so with such an attitude of selfish flippancy. It was all made doubly worse because I had recognised and acknowledged that this small stand of trees held a particular quality of slender beauty that gave me pause to still, listen and experience grace. They had spoken to my heart and I had broken covenant with them. Some days later I was returning from Llanberis through the woods, after dark, and my path took me through the birch copse. Unconsciously trying to evade the gnawing sense of my wrongdoing, I shoved my way through the trees, roughly brushing the small branches away from my face. For the first time ever outdoors at night in the woods, I felt frightened by an opaque hostility, a distinct feeling of threat and enmity. I never saw what hit me, but it felt like the weighted cords of a lash and, crying out, I was sent sprawling into the snow clutching my face. In the weeks that followed, I avoided the birch trees and I never mentioned the incident to my friends. I was ashamed and I knew I had done something that, by my own standards, was unworthy. My casual felling of that young tree belied my deeper knowing. It held a harsh mirror to my eyes, showing me the unavoidable truth of my dishonest dialogue with sacredness. I felt diminished by the precise reflection of the man I was. A week later, I tried to make amends, but it was only in January 2009 when I revisited these trees that I felt at peace with this fragment of my past. My companion in those earlier days was a very affable female Labrador called Meg. When she died, I buried her in this grove of trees, for she, too, loved to sit among them and pass the time of day.

Along a track and across a couple of fields, there is a property called Cae Mabon that, even in 1978, I secretly coveted. It intrigued me, and on one occasion I crept close and spied it out. Eric Maddern, who built a beautiful and enchanting eco-retreat centre here, bought it some years later.[31] It was here, with Eric and some of the community, that I stayed on Sunday, 18 January, enjoying their warm and genial hospitality. The moon was in its last quarter and snow was forecast. My sleep was troubled, a jumble of shadowed images jostling for prominence. Disturbed memories, fragments of disjointed conversation and uneasy repetitive cycles of thought that led nowhere and provided no resolution. Together with friends, Eric constructed a very atmospheric roundhouse, designed in a manner similar to those found in late Iron-Age Britain.

It has a very striking entrance and, like all the roundhouses I have visited, evokes powerful memories and exciting images of how our people once lived. When I was visiting in 2009, the roundhouse at Cae Mabon was used as an evocative gathering place for many different groups. I have visited a number of roundhouses constructed to various designs understood to replicate the evolving history of our Bronze and Iron Age dwelling places. In most of them I have felt touched by magic while sitting around the central fire in the flame-lit interior; yet,

---

[31] www.caemabon.co.uk.

in most but not all, I feel sadness at the lack of a consistently held intention as a place of deep listening and mindful enquiry. They hint at something that was once some part of my heart, without then standing and naming themselves as such. They provide a space that can be negotiated, compliant to the whimsy of whoever occupies it, submissive to careless boundaries, perforated and waiting for direction. In this way they offer a very stringent metaphor for the man that I have been, and the man I chose to set aside when I stood in ceremony, naked under the moon and pledged my journey in this lifetime. Standing in the roundhouse early that evening – seeing, feeling, smelling and dreaming the texture of an ancient tribal people – I had a bodily experience of the Welsh *hiraeth*.[32]

> There is hiraeth in the sea and the long-living mountain
> There is hiraeth in silence and in song
> In the murmur of water on its eternal journey
> In the hours of sunset and in flames of fire
> Gently it whispers its moan in the wind
> And the wind replies with sorrow in the sedge
> Waking the echo of an echo in the rush
> And the memory of a memory in the heart
>
> Mae hiraeth yn y mor a'r mynydd maith
> Mae hireath mewn distawrwydd ac mewn can
> Mewn murmur dyfroedd ar dragywydd daith
> Yn oriau'ar machlud ac yn fflamau'r tan
> Ond mwynaf yn y gwynt y dwed ei gwyn
> A thristaf yn yr hesg y cwyna'r gwynt
> Gan ddeffro adlais adlais yn y brwyn
> Ac yn y galon, atgof atfot gynt[33]

I am very impressed with my smartphone, and I marvel at the silent, gliding stealth of the hybrid car that now transports my

---

[32] An uncontainable longing for the landscape of home that is lost and will never return.

[33] Welsh, translation by Iona Hannagan Lewis.

family on missions around Devon, but I doubt I will ever escape the sense that, outside of stone, water, sinew, blade, fire, herb and breath, everything feels synthetic in comparison. The felt impact of Eric's thatched Iron Age roundhouse, set in a glade among oak trees on the northern valley hillside of Llyn Padarn, the tumbling vigour of the stream, leaping and swirling its way to the lake below – some of the same sounds that have resonated in this valley for thousands of years. The occasional flurry of sleet, dancing and shifting in the way of birds flocking. Standing in the woods where, three decades earlier, I had begun a new journey – the animal that I am knew these things and called them familiar. I have always felt between worlds, and that evening I knew the truth of this feeling without knowing the implication.

Day 17: Sunday, 18 January

The following morning, once more packed and ready, with Gyre making small, sun-wise twists as my hand exerted pressure on the spiral of his honeysuckle-constricted curves, I turned northward. I began to seek a way uphill, across the shoulder of the mountain Elidir, and then on down to Bethesda in the next valley. Within minutes, I was enveloped in a snowstorm with all familiar landmarks erased, a bewitched landscape that sang me deeper into its inscrutable folds of subtle enticement. Behind me, the roundhouse gathered a soft white robe around its sloping shoulders and, crone-like, passed word ahead to the mountain.

***

Close to the time of her death, my maternal grandmother spoke to her daughter. 'Do not waste your life on the church', she said. After years of service to the Methodist Church and dedicated social work, she had a sense that she had caged her intelligence, curiosity and vitality inside something that was smaller than the life that was about to leave her. She never said as much to me, but, if she had, even at seven years old, I think I would have agreed, unconditionally. Leaving the spiritual clarity of grass, trees and newly dug earth to enter the sterile, dusty tedium of tuneless hymns and monotonous sermons did not feel like a step towards the divine to me. It felt like slavery and a denial of truth. Nature awoke in me a transcendent acknowledgement of life's implicit spirituality. This illumination owed nothing to my own efforts; it was given to me in the same way that Idun brought the casket of apples to the gods and goddesses of Asgard.[34] It was not until I became sexually mature, and the chemistry of my body and mind began to change, that I apprehended some part of the complex weave that would have to be untangled if I were to walk the slow journey home. A dawning awareness of the atavistic tug that connects us to our ancient soul, still buried deep in the embodied memory of our species. This archaic, and largely disowned, aspect of our humanity has been a source of great concern to many visionaries of a better world. Frightened, even appalled, at our subterranean animal nature, there have been endless efforts directed at constraining, punishing, shaming, ignoring, disowning and banning this molten core of our raw interior. None have been successful. Whether we attempt to focus exclusively on divine light, seek communion through prayer, beg forgiveness or hum the sanitised dilutions of indigenous chants, the shadow of the eschewed primitive will always find a way in. Laws, social mores, traffic regulations and human resource departments all fall at the same hurdle. Banished to the perimeter of our conscious awareness, the phenomenal power of this eruptive force becomes dangerous and unpredictable. It seems that emphasising one aspect of our nature at the expense of the other invokes the very tsunami that we were hoping to eliminate. Exalting the light invites in the dark. When the full sphere of our ancient and modern self is invited to integrate, and we reach out to the demons that are crouching in the penumbra of half-light surrounding our home fire, perhaps there is an opportunity

---

[34] Roger Lancelyn Green, *The Saga of Asgard* (London, Penguin, 1960), p. 55.

for wholeness. Every time we reach for the stars and cease to attend to our feet, we become vulnerable to the jealousy of that which is dishonoured and excluded. Only deeming light, goodness, kindness and perfection as holy informs the fierce creative vortex of our primordial ancestry that it is not welcome. This uncontrollable, vast and unknowable ocean of power will then tear the fabric of our little dream, and forcibly take its seat at the table before vomiting on the fine linen of our dinner party and cavorting its demonic jig. Nothing on this Earth or beyond will withhold it. Feeding the myth of the heroic leader who will guide us to salvation, whether a religious figure or a business executive, will always eventually lead to tears. Romanticising our partner until they become a goddess or god will provide us with moments of ecstasy and a millennium of sorrow. Living in a rural idyll, we imagine that, by virtue of our surroundings, we are by association righteous, good and beyond reproach – when in the cold light of day our actions speak of bigotry, ignorance and vindictiveness. In whatever form the romantic myth constellates, the outcome will always be the same. I know about these things because I am susceptible to the charm of substituting myth for wholeness. The root cause is the existential fear and loneliness we experienced when we turned our backs on gratitude and substituted it with greed. Wisdom and compassion do not turn their backs on the wild hinterland of our inheritance, but nature, indigeny and the intoxicating story of our tribal past is potentially as harmful, if lifted to the sun on the wings of the Icarus myth.

It is with horror that I first became aware of the attempted appropriation of the term 'indigenous' by far-right groups, looking to embed their fascist, racist and anti-Semitic ideology into the romance of tribal myth; yet, this has been going on for some time, and to sickening effect. It was my mother who first intimated a connection between the history and ideas I was so enthusiastically extolling and the Nazi regime's extermination of six million Jews in the Second World War.

**

Arminius was a tribal chieftain of the Cherusci people. For some years he was an auxiliary in the Roman Army and, no doubt, gained many useful insights into the strengths and limitations of their military arts. For reasons undocumented, Arminius turned his back on the legions, returned to the Cherusci and led his people against Rome. Deep inside the Teutoberg forest in 9 CE, he successfully orchestrated the annihilation of three Roman legions under the generalship of Publius Quinctilius Varus. Another Roman commander, Germanicus, whose uncle was Emperor Tiberius, was sent to punish Arminius and the Cherusci, which, after some years, he accomplished. The Roman historian Tacitus recorded some of this history and, in doing so, sowed the idealised romantic seeds that were later mythologised by Conrad Celtis in fifteenth-century Germany. This poet and orator invoked a vision of sylvan simplicity and virtue, and the uncorrupted moral strength of Germany's ancient forest-dwelling tribal people. The myth took root and grew stronger; from this emerged the story of the fatherland, and a glorious destiny for the 'pure' ancient lineage that could, once again, stand proud and assume its rightful place within the leaders of the world. As Hitler manoeuvred his way to power, together with his closest aides, he promulgated the myth further and deeper into the imagination of a people floundering in the bewildered aftermath of the First World War; the rest… is history. It is no wonder that we, in Europe, still find refuge in the lofty, rational world of Plato and Aristotle. Yet it is a compromised hiding place that is consistently proven to be inadequate by the fact that, in addition to mind, we also have bodies, emotions and the inscrutable mystery of soul and spirit, yearning to be included. Logos without mythos offers a dreary world stripped of meaning, which leaves us bereft, calling alone in colourless terrain while clutching the last bag of shopping to our denuded heart. The celebrated author and thinker Karen Armstrong writes:

> We are myth-making creatures and, during the twentieth century, we saw some very destructive modern myths, which have ended in massacre and genocide. These myths have

failed because they do not meet the criterion of the Axial Age. They have not been infused with the spirit of compassion, respect for the sacredness of all life, or with what Confucius called 'leaning'. These destructive mythologies have been narrowly racial, ethnic, denominational and egotistic, an attempt to exalt the self by demonising the other ... We need myths that help us venerate the earth as sacred once again, instead of merely using it as a 'resource'. This is crucial because unless there is some kind of spiritual revolution that is able to keep abreast of our technological genius, we will not save our planet.[35]

With snow crunching underfoot, I made my uncertain way along footpaths and lanes, gradually gaining height and ascending the shoulder of Elidir. Each cautious step took me deeper into a strange and unfamiliar world. I became conscious of feelings that I have experienced on occasion in the past, and I have no name for these feelings, except 'premonition'. Something extraordinary happened to me that day, and I still do not fully understand what it was.

For a while, it seemed that my whole day's journey would be made in the vortex of a snowstorm. The wind was whipping across the mountain, sending great swirls of snowflakes dipping and swooping, like shoals of fish, across the cramped stonewalled fields. In a very short while it was banking against the sides of the lanes in softly contoured drifts, and I found myself beginning to pay careful attention to my route, in case I lost my bearings and had to try and find my way back to Eric's. Visibility was reduced to about twenty-five metres and the storm was still growing in intensity. Head down against the driving wind and snow, I was relying on my vague memory of this land, which I had once known quite well. During the first few weeks of my arrival in Wales in the late '70s, I had attended a party held in a cottage on Bigil – a rocky hilltop, which, at this point, was somewhere to my left and not more than one mile distant. 'Party' doesn't really conjure images appropriate to the bacchanalian frenzy of crazed hedonism that was throbbing and gyrating in that small traditional Welsh cottage. At one point, reeling and intoxicated, I lurched out of the cottage's front door and straight into the embrace of a snowstorm. It was, of course, magnificently beautiful; a snowstorm the like of which I had never seen before. It was also hideously cold and, stripped down for dancing, I might as well have been naked for all the benefit I derived from the shreds of clothing that whipped and lashed dementedly against my exposed body. Needless to say, I registered neither the cold nor the inadvisability of remaining outside and, awed by the columns of dervish snowflakes that spun, pirouetted and leapt before me, I had the idea of finding the highest mound and standing in the most exposed spot as I sought to absorb the storm into my soaring spirit. A few steps later, a couple of turns and then, looking skywards with outstretched arms, I began to register the ferocious arctic cold that had stripped the heat from my flesh and was now rapidly penetrating deeper to the core. I looked around and could not see anything, except the black of night and the beguiling snowflakes dancing in front of my eyes. A few moments of ineffective floundering, wrong turns and bewildered staring were followed by the reassertion of a strong desire to live, and the massive effort required to apply my emphatically diminished, rational mind to the task of working out where the cottage was most likely to be located. On the first attempt, and with the timely intervention of good fortune, the cottage appeared as an opaque, hulking grey in my infernally snow-infatuated world. I found the front door, fell inside and returned to Alice in Wonderland, not emerging again until the following morning.

Memories of this kind allowed moments of grim humour as I pressed on, but they did not last long. I felt weighted and uneasy, unsure about the arising feelings of portent that slithered in the deeper recesses of an older, lizard mind. Gyre maintained a mien of stoic indifference, resolutely maintaining rhythm and distance from my faltering confidence. The cottages were thinning out, and I became concerned that I was gaining too much height; I worried that I might walk my way towards Marchlyn Mawr Lake by inadvertently turning east, and heading directly up the mountain. As I rounded another corner, I heard a faint bellowing and screeching in the distance. I could not identify the sound, and after a few moments it receded, once more giving way to the dull white world of cloud-enshrouded snow. Again, the world contracted to the small sphere of my laboured breath, the tiny squeaks of compressed snow and to the monotonous crunch of Gyre's pace-keeping. As I came to the bottom of a slope where the road forked, with one track leading uphill and another easing away to the left and to more level ground, a car came hurtling out of the translucent grey, heading downhill and straight towards me. It leapt at me, ferociously lunging across the hillside, full of rage and indiscriminate, snarling its hatred and reaching for me. Enveloped in a world that felt entirely disconnected from ordinary reality, the noise, the snowflakes, the insane squealing and the shock of surprise, I froze, watching. Only intermittently under control, the car spun and dived its way down the lane as a frenzied and scarcely visible driver wrestled with the wheel. I caught a glimpse of his face, a momentary image of blankness, like a face with no features – just the smooth stretch of skin, drawn too tight over an overly large skull. At the last moment, the car wrenched its way around the curve and dived into the gloom, as it ploughed into banks of snow and began braking. Wheels spinning, engine screaming, the driver forced it into reverse, backed up, smashed it into first gear and, with the rear end of the car flailing from side to side, shot away, back up the way it had come.

Stillness; the quiet of snow and the wind easing. Almost without thinking, I began to walk again, confused, upset and disorientated, feeling the shocking impact of the blow that never landed. I approached the point where the road forked left and, with some relief, turned my back on the violent images that jostled in the recesses of my jumbled mind. Again came the roaring clamour, a shriek of metal abrading metal and the tumbling roar of an avalanche. In my bones, I knew that the driver sought to frighten me. He knew where I was, he knew the risks and, without restraint, scarcely in control, he came on anyway. The weeks of walking, the dreaming, the proximate spirit world, the delicacy of knowing that I was nearing home, induced an unconditional refusal to give way or show my fear. Suffusing throughout my body, the chilled bloodstream of defiant refusal. 'I will not have this stolen from me.' Seconds divided by milliseconds and time stretched, whipping like wind-tormented telephone wires, moaning and desiring to snap. I felt the driver's eyes on my retreating back, the jarring dissonance of one world colliding with another, desolate, adrift and disconnected. I could not bear to engage with this intrusion into my dreaming ceremony; it would have felt like an acknowledgement of defeat. All I could see and feel was the assailing torment of being tested by spirits, who existed in worlds parallel to my own. The ungovernable, demonic powers of chaos, un-held, would snatch the tiller from our grasp and send the ship cavorting on waves that have no mercy. Spirits, willed into their rightful place, can become wells of creativity and potency. In the interior halls of my soul, I uttered a silent declaration of independence to the unseen ghosts of the mountain and the tribal memory of peoples long gone: 'I will not budge.'

Stillness. Soft snow, a down quilt laid upon the frigid land. The car came to a halt a few metres behind me, skewed broadside and briefly motionless. Eyes ahead, I kept walking. The engine gunned and growled as it made preparation for the short return journey uphill. I did not care. I was already gone and, bonded with Gyre, I reached into the netherworld one step further. Somehow, I assumed a return to normal – a swift resumption of the familiar patterning that filled the spaces of my day – but it was not to be. I had walked through something and everything had changed. Once again, the drumbeat of footfall and staff resumed and, charged with energy, alert to the engulfing mystery of invisible frequencies, I found myself emerging onto the broad saddle of the hilltop as it curved around the mountain before descending into the valley below. The snow had almost stopped, and light suffused a pewter sky. Everywhere the land lay sleeping beneath a blanket of newly fallen snow. Every sharp edge, crag and angular form was stroked into a soft camber of temporary compliance, and my eyes were drawn to the horizon. A mile distant, I could see a lone figure walking towards me. Perhaps the harsh encounter to which I had so recently been exposed had animated my senses, but from the first moment of noticing this figure, I became watchful and wary. Once again, I had a strange sense of time, alternatively elongating and contracting. At the same time, the figure seemed to be rushing towards me, yet scarcely moving. I felt unprepared and simultaneously impatient with the deep foreboding that clutched at my stomach. Trying to shake off my discomfort, I attempted to engage Gyre in one of our accustomed bouts of friendly banter, but he was unresponsive, stiff and strangely reticent. I had the feeling that he, too, was uncomfortable and inwardly preparing for the unexpected. I looked again, and this time I could make out more detail. Nothing I saw assuaged my unease. There was something distinctly odd in the way this person moved – an aura of disembodiment, lostness and sorrow. Ever since setting out from Cae Mabon and following the footpaths and tracks that took me up onto the hill, ever since the snowstorm had thrown its mantle across the fields and hidden me from view, I had felt a shift in reality, a sense of walking beyond and a place in-between. Every step became more difficult, every step a conflicted dialogue between my rational and superstitious minds. I looked again. This time I could just make out that the figure – a woman, I guessed – was seemingly looking from side to side, as if searching for something. A couple of hundred yards now separated us and, as the distance between us closed, her movements became more obviously rhythmic. With every step, she was alternately looking from one side of the snow-covered lane to the other. There was no deviation in her movement, not the slightest pause or catch in the gliding swing of her head to suggest that her eyes were seeing. They felt sightless, looking yet seeing nothing. She walked in the middle of the lane, as I did, and, stifling the panicky, rising confusion that welled inside me, I began to prepare myself for an acknowledgement. We were going to pass so close to each other that it would have felt bizarre not to say something. I also assumed that she, like me, would make some move to ease sideways as we passed alongside so as to share the inconvenience of moving into deeper snow. We drew close and I opened my mouth to speak, but after the first syllable nothing came out.

'Mag…?!'

I swerved to the right, wading into the banked snow as I realised that she was not going to alter her course. For a brief second I looked into her face, and I saw the noticeably masculine features of a woman I had known a long time ago: Maggie. The eyes, head-swing and stride of the woman never faltered as she glided past me, maintaining the constant swerve of a downward glance that shifted from left to right, right to left. In the fraction of time I saw her face, I first felt flooded with relief and then with shock because I thought I recognised her, but as I began to mouth her name I was frozen into silence by the woman's uninhabited, unseeing eyes and the knowledge that, for her, I did not exist. One step past and, again, I reeled from the prescient knowing that I recognised this face, but this time it was a face that I had only ever seen once in my life. It was the face of a woman that I had peered at through the fractured glass of a shattered windscreen, as blood washed my face and hers. The dead face that stared into the dark night after the tumult of a car crash, close by the southeast shoreline of the Isle of Mona. It was the face of the woman who, many years past, had deliberately driven her car at mine and thereby fulfilled a promise made shortly before, to her female lover: that she would kill herself on the first car that came towards her. Me, as that turned out to be.

I swivelled round, staring at the retreating figure as it continued its passage as before; the same monotonous swing of the head, the same achingly lonely, forlorn and abandoned quality. Tears broke from my eyes and I sobbed for something and somebody I never knew, or perhaps I sobbed for me; I don't know. I was alone again, and unsure of everything. All I knew was that I could see in front of me the splayed footprints of someone who was clearly angling their body from one side to another. For the next half-mile or so I walked in their footsteps. It was as if they were the footsteps of the figure, now soon to disappear behind me, walking into a death landscape. I knew that I was walking into life.

The light-infused pewter sky had given way to the sun and I was walking in sunshine. Words that I had copied down in a notebook, when I was eighteen and still at school, rushed to my assistance.

And life is light, and colour, and warmth, and a striving evermore for these.[36]

Another couple of miles, and I arrived at the home of some dear friends, Sheila and Mark. In the comfort of their hospitality, I sheltered another night. At one point in the evening, I shared what had happened to me with Sheila, telling her that I thought I had passed Maggie on the mountain, and mentioning her resemblance to the woman who had died in the car accident many years before.

'But Mac, Maggie's dead. She killed herself a few years ago...'

We stared at each other. I was speechless, uncomprehending, only knowing that, on the flanks of the mountain, Elidir, in a frozen land of snow and ice, I had found my way into a mystery – an assignation with fate. In those few hours, I had entered a

---

[36] Julian Grenfell. First published in *The Times* the day after Grenfell's death, on 27 May 1915, written on the battlefield in Flanders in April of the same year.

netherworld. I touched my toe to the ocean of sorrow and ennui that infuses our human story, and yet by no means bestrides it. In some way, I feel that our species lives on this Earth like the woman that I met on the mountain: lost, drowning in the sorrow of a failed promise to the mother who gave us life in the first place. Wandering trails, searching for home, acutely lonely because we choose to imagine ourselves more than we can ever be – or should, indeed, ever desire to be. Lost to ourselves and lost to life. Existing in a netherworld that is neither life nor death. Held in suspension, inert, numb, confused and beyond the pale. It is choosing life that will bring us out of the netherworld. It is choosing to take the advice of those few remnants of indigenous peoples who, still attending to the mother, advise that the purpose of a human life is 'to care for all living things.'

Stripped, bathed and tired beyond the means of one night's rest to restore my body, I set out for Mona the following morning.

Day 18: Monday, 19 January

I emerged from the mountain valley that now provides the cleft through which the A5 trunk road passes and began my slow descent to the sea. With so many roads, cars, trucks, buildings and people, it is easy to have almost no sense of the landscape we inhabit. Everything competes to grab our attention. Only the land itself holds a quality of poise and still watchfulness, observing our frenetic egotism without comment, standing in dignity. Walking towards the sea along a cycle track that had usurped the old railway line, for which the land had been incised and graded, I could feel the massive presence of the mountains behind me. Acrid and unfamiliar to me for many years, the thick cloying smell of coal smoke, the triumphant vigour of buddleia shrubs awaiting the spring and, somewhere far behind, the sound of the voices of men whose labour had created this railway. Before long I was in Bangor, the largest town I had passed through since Hereford. I had lived in Bangor for some years in the early '80s but, moving through the streets and along routes that I once knew well, I had no feelings of connection or relationship. I was, once again, walking in the land of cast-aside plastic bottles, with their inane insignia begging the brief attention of idle money. One lay prostrate and impotent in the gutter, exhorting those who passed by to 'Excel'. Everything shifted once again as I approached the bridge that spans the Menai Straits and caught my first glimpse of Mona. Fringed with oak trees right to the water's edge, subtle, withheld, now masked and protected from the banality of eyes that only see the surface. Mona, the island for which I had been searching these last few weeks of frozen cold; at intervals, gazing up to the sky for one of two stars to navigate my way. This island, once the last bastion of a dying culture and home to a wisdom tradition that fell to a power whose ambitions reached even to the furthest ends of the world. Mona, a name that had inspired fierce loyalty and stark terror in equal measure; a myth in its own time; the anthem of a tribal people and one of the great repositories of Celtic law, knowledge, ceremony and culture. An island library in the oral tradition, perhaps equalling those of antiquity that also fell to fire and sword. Mona, the cradle of my awakening soul, the place where I decided not to discount my own incipient spiritual awakening, but instead chose to scribe a circle in the soil and declare myself indigenous to this Earth. Mona, where I made some of my most stupid mistakes and most intelligent choices; the island where I heard the echo of an ancient soul awakening, and shoved bashfulness aside, that I might not feel ashamed of declining the first honour that I have had the privilege to hold.

'Doesn't get much better than this, does it?'

She was bent, frail and pushing a shopping trolley; an elderly and very tiny woman. I looked at her, unable to speak, but nodding my agreement and loving her with all my heart. She swung to the left as I went right, and, holding my black dreaming stone in my left hand and Gyre in my right, I walked the bridge to my island destination.

That morning, I found comfort and rest in the anonymity of a small, comfortable café in Menai Bridge. I decided to rest awhile before pressing on to Llanfairpwllgwyngyll and walking southwest along the coast to a conference that I was scheduled to attend that evening. I was not feeling chatty, but I had grown used to unexpected and significant meetings with strangers. After a few words across tables, I invited one of the other café-loungers to have lunch with me. Without pause, we segued from friendly trivialities to profound encounter. I cannot recall her name, but she had been travelling to the Ukraine with her partner and their small son. We talked, shared dreams, laughed and periodically lapsed into silence. I left the café with a heightened sense of just how open and tender I was: the elderly lady, my café friend, Mona. That afternoon I walked along the road to Newborough Warren, passing the turning to Bryn Celli Ddu, the burial mound that was my final destination. I was not ready, and the conference was probably already in full swing. Satisfied that I had fulfilled the requirements of my journey as regards walking, I arranged a taxi to take me to Newborough Warren at the extreme southwest point of Mona. This time there was no internal conflict as to who should benefit from the ride. Together with Gyre, I dragged my backpack into the plush interior of the taxi and rediscovered the exquisite pleasure of a very soft, yielding seat. It was a bewildering experience. In thirty minutes, we travelled the same distance that I would normally walk in half a day. In my weakened state, and reacquainted to the comforts of twenty-first-century living, I was abruptly reminded of the benefits that science, engineering and human innovation have heaped upon us. It may well be that a soft, plush seat, held within a petrol-powered car, is an old and somewhat compromised invention, but I had no room for anything except gratitude. This was closely followed by regret, when I was obliged to clamber out on to the road and watch as the taxi retreated back the way we had come.

With the sun dipping towards the horizon behind me, I walked through the pine forest, towards the sea. Burrowing into the trees, I made my camp, collected fuel and began to settle down for the night. Shortly after I had lit the birch bark and seen the first tiny flames lick and twine the tinder, I stiffened and froze. A forest ranger's 4x4 vehicle was softly creeping along the track. Again, the familiar rush of adrenaline, the intense commitment to secrecy and remaining undetected. The low-pitched, feral snarl of a potentially compromised position, and the uneasy proximity of wild to tame; I shielded the small fire with my body, pulled the camouflaged tarp over my head, and folded myself to the ground. I felt eyes sweeping the trees and the murmur of the engine passing by. There is something so profoundly nourishing about eluding capture, stalking quarry and moving unseen through the enemy camp, erasing tracks. I was unhappy with the location I had chosen and resolved to move camp early the following morning. Meanwhile, the conference was fully underway above me in the canopy of the trees; over several acres of forest, hundreds of ravens.

Day 19: Tuesday, 20 January

A Native American elder once told me that the ravens were the teachers of natural law. In 2003, standing in the big meadow at Embercombe, near the stone circle, I witnessed a conspiracy of about sixty ravens approaching our valley from Dartmoor, and then wheeling around until they were describing a great circle above our land. Performing their distinctive aerial stunts, soaring and all the while communicating with each other, they were like nubs of airborne charcoal, scribing a ring of hieroglyphs in the sky. The folklore surrounding these magical creatures predictably associates them with evil and death, hence the group descriptions being a 'conspiracy' or an 'unkindness' of ravens. Looking up at them that day, marvelling at their playfulness, sense of community and complex language, I felt only wonder; grace. It felt like a blessing. To be on the Isle of Mona five years later, and sleeping beneath a congress of these birds, just 200 metres from the sea, was very special. This was once the second-largest raven roost in the world and, at its height, was populated by more than 2000 birds. I lay on my back and, at intervals, looked up to see a raven peering down at me, apparently unconcerned by my presence, but clearly aware and interested.

'What's he doing now?' That seemed to be a recurring question from some others, followed by a commentary that was mostly speculative and make-believe. That night, as the wind wailed and groaned in the treetops, the ocean beat against the ragged shoreline and the ravens continued their interminable council, I flitted between sleep and wakefulness; worlds converging, time bending, shapes shifting. Before I finally sank beneath the waves of the dream world, I had the passing thought that perhaps the druids never did leave Mona. Bards, healers, intellectuals and shamans, the lines separating raven from druid seemed insubstantial, a trick of the light, a cloud passing before the moon.

Native peoples around the world have devised and practised ceremonies incorporating fasting, solitude and prayer for millennia. Ever since Native American spiritual teachings became popularised in the '60s and '70s, and elements of their ceremonial traditions lodged in the imagination of a generation seeking renewal, we have heard tell of the vision quest. Although most traditional world religions have also included teachings that incorporated the value of solitary contemplation in wild country, the vision quest of Native American origins was perceived by many to offer a direct, unmediated conversation with spirit. In my late twenties I was one of those young people. When I began learning from my Native American mentors, cushioned between the many excruciating confrontations I experienced were times when, seated around a fire, stories were shared and I could grasp a brief, intoxicating respite. I recall the stories of people going on vision quests in times when our world was not spinning quite so fast. These stories would tell of a young woman or man requesting a ceremony and making thorough, detailed and disciplined preparation over weeks, or perhaps months. The day would arrive when they had to start their journey to the medicine man or woman, who would be holding their ceremony. These people were not necessarily living nearby and sometimes the journey might take weeks. In the comfortable, shadowed safety of the circle around the fire, I would imagine these journeys; days following days, following weeks and sometimes even months. The scorching sun and ever-present need for vigilance; the vast celestial nights; the storms and the solitude; the memory of the old journey songs guiding the seeker as they pressed far beyond the tribe's familiar land; the mishaps, wonders, misgivings and epiphanies. In these stories, the journey to the place where the vision quest was to be held was an essential part of the preparation, an essential part of the ceremony. Once arriving at the medicine chief's home, the young seeker might spend several days cleaning, cooking and helping in all the ways useful to the mundane life of ordinary living. Further preparation would be made and then, eventually, the ceremony would take place. Afterwards, the whole process would be reversed until finally, heated, hammered, cooled and flexed on the anvil forge of spiritual enquiry and physical endeavour, the woman or man would rejoin their people, renewed and also changed. For us, it is different. We finish work with another flurry of emails, grab the suitcase, miss the train, catch the next, wait in the rain for a taxi, get stuck in traffic and arrive late, missing dinner. One week later, and sometimes much sooner, we check in to the office again, switch on the computer and – chin up – face the consequences of taking our lives seriously. It is not easy to cram our rewilding soul into the unyielding cage of school holidays, mortgage repayments and the unreasonable expectations of colleagues, friends, partners, children, parents and the family pet.

My journey to Mona was not a vision quest, but it was a ceremony, and here on the shores of the Celtic Sea, I entered once more the between-world space that I call the netherworld. It is not a land in which I would wish to linger, but it is familiar to me and, in some way that I do not understand, I am called to attend this place from time to time, to make representation. The waves were some way out and a cold wind scoured the tidal flats, sending flurries of sand scurrying towards the dunes. Everything was grey and stretched, like old skin over bones. The forest behind me swelled and shrank, as gusts came cavorting off the foaming waves and hurled themselves against the banked trees. Most of the ravens had left at dawn but a few remained, riding on the billowing strength of an unseen power. This is how it is with wind; we cannot see it, only that which it moves. In observing the effect of the wind, we imagine we see it, but we do not. It is inscrutable, authoritative and self-willed. The netherworld is a world of lostness, wandering spirits and homelessness. It is a bowl of tears. In it are gathered all the lost souls, never-endingly searching for a place of rest and peace. It is a wasteland of broken promises and forgotten dreams – the dreary repository of squandered gifts. For all its quality of forlorn desolation, its timeless nature and the pounding echo of eternity, it is also home to the first revelation, the tiny spark from which came the first breath. It is the silent howling of Auschwitz, when all the visitors have gone and the grey night descends. It is the desecration from which the phoenix may yet rise again. I held the Iceni chariot ring to the wind and bathed it in the sea. I called to my relatives, the pyramid of elders upon whose shoulders I stand. I roared the names of our tribes to the ocean, and looked out over the crests of waves that, for millions of years, have danced to shorelines of this land and others. I remembered Pangaea, the mega-continent that once bestrode the Earth in the early Mesozoic era, and the journey of countless life forms as the Earth spoke with the grandparents and conjured legions of life forms to step forward. I felt the presence of the first hominids standing next to me and knew them to be my relatives. I found myself hurtling back in time and standing among the ancient ones who had called me on this journey. They, too, had knowledge of the netherworld, for it is here that they were left when the last oak grove fell and the last scream reverberated out across the serried waves. Held in columns of spume, and dashed upon the rocks, their dreams were buried under the assumption that 'might bestows right'. Beached and crumpled, bloodless and sightless, staring into a time beyond, as armies march to new battlefields, a lone woman sows grain in the darkly turned earth of an abandoned field, that there might be food for her family next year. I knew that I had undertaken the journey from my birthplace to this isle of dreams in order to stitch just one thread across a torn, gaping lesion that separates our modern society from the homeland of ancient belonging, and kinship with nature. One thread to accompany many others in once again weaving the cloth from which all human spiritual experience finds its wellspring; reverence for the earth, reverence for life.

I am tired of fighting. Our Chiefs are killed; Looking Glass is dead, Ta Hool Shute is dead. The old men are all dead. It is the young men who say yes or no. He who led on the young men is dead. It is cold, and we have no blankets; the little children are freezing to death. My people, some of them, have run away to the hills, and have no blankets, no food. No one knows where they are – perhaps freezing to death. I want to have time to look for my children, and see how many of them I can find. Maybe I shall find them among the dead. Hear me, my Chiefs! I am tired; my heart is sick and sad. From where the sun now stands I will fight no more forever.[37]

Day 20: Tuesday, 21 January

A final inspection to check that my camp was rendered invisible, a few words of appreciation, a wave to the ravens, a walk down to the water's edge and a prayer offered to the rising tide. I turned away from the sea and began walking up through the woods to Newborough. I was on my way to Bryn Celli Ddu burial chamber, and the end of my ceremony. It had been my

---

[37] Hin-mut-too-yah-lat-kekht (Thunder Rolling Down the Mountain) on the occasion of his surrender to General Nelson A. Miles on 5 October 1877.

intention to spend my last night inside the mound but, even before I got there, I was not sure if it felt right. The profound cold, walking many miles, the trail of fires by which I had sat and warmed my aching body and soul, the netherworld; all this, and so much more, had left me very tender, sensitive and weary. On a whim, I changed plan and, with the help of a bus and a taxi, I returned to Menai Bridge, where I spent several hours in the café I had visited two days earlier. Singly, and in pairs, various elderly women visited. I thought I had returned for physical comfort, and the opportunity to write and reflect. Instead, I found myself participating in multiple, animated, humorous and stimulating conversations with people who were at least fifteen years my senior. One woman in particular had a glowing quality that filled the café with radiance. I was entranced, captivated by her vitality, wit and open-hearted curiosity. When she and the others left I sat alone, contrasting the worlds I had experienced in the last few days. I realised then, as I know now, that essential to the life I wish to lead is the encompassing breadth that spans the sacred and the profane, suffering and rapture, desolation and abundance, anguish and joy. The book of life that I read sets out no limits on the extremes that accompany our human experience on this Earth. With every mile that I covered, as I wended my way among the valleys and hills of west England and Wales, I witnessed beauty, generosity, kindness and grace, alive and present in a continuous cascade of unfolding love. I also witnessed intense pain, and a cruel indifference to suffering – a sociopathic megalomania that orates the philosophy of I, me, mine and self. Some believe that our ape species evolves towards wisdom, but I remain unconvinced. The prodigious brain grows in power, and evidence of genius abounds, yet in the 'developed' countries of our civilised world, we have mostly found ourselves unable to agree even the simplest notions of sharing, respect and collaboration. Knowing what makes us happy, and fully cognisant of that which makes us sad, we unerringly choose the latter. Why wouldn't we? The god to whom we make obeisance has set fear in the centre of his doctrinal theology and, to this, we kneel in submission. Acknowledging that it was time to complete my mission, I shouldered my backpack and set out for Bryn Celli Ddu. It seems that only when pressed by circumstance do we discover what we love and value. At a very personal level it has been like this for me, and I have met many hundreds more who have negotiated a similar journey. It could be that, squeezed to the cliff-edge, we will unfurl wings and risk flying. It is a choice and it could be ours.

One hour before dusk, and I stand inside the henge, before the passage-chamber's entrance. I sing a song that was given to me in 1984 by my Native American mentors and I prepare myself to enter the passageway.

In my right hand I hold the Iceni ring. Gyre is outside, close by the replica of a pattern stone, with its serpentine and spiral shapes. To the druids of Mona in 60 CE, the henge, along with the passage tomb, was already ancient, footprints speaking of ancestors long past. At the end of the passageway, there is a polygonal chamber in which stands a single, tall, rounded stone. I recall the discovery of the human ear bone found buried near this place. I am reminded of the underground kiva, within which I once stood in ceremony with Tracker and Moon Panther. During the latter stages of that ceremony I was graced with a vision, revealing to me the spirit essence that inhabits our bodies, and which, at death, flies free.

The journey along the passage is the journey from Malvern to Mona; the journey from womb to birth; from life to death. It is the Invisible Path, the tunnel of fire and the column of life-force, which once erupted from the base of my spine to the top of my head, curving back around to my crotch. It is what awaits my last breath; Bifrost, ancient bridge of many colours. Now, standing in the chamber and seeking to finish this task well, I speak into the shadowed cave of the longing that has fuelled this migration into soul. Hand trembling, and in language hauled from obscured depths, I honour the indigenous people of the world; the tribal people of this land, our trees, mountains, springs, rivers and lakes. I shout out the names of old chiefs and promise that this is only a beginning. I speak on behalf of all those who know the pain of disconnection and disenfranchisement; of the oppressed and the poor, the numb and the unhelpfully wealthy. I thank all those who have fought for freedom, prayed for freedom and planted seed for freedom. I thank the scientists who have spared so many lives and opened the doors to worlds only imagined. Messily, without structure and certain only in my sincerity, I tried to give my heart to the ear bone and be heard. Be heard saying 'thank-you'. This man, this archaic soul, this 'between-worlds' human, who, since first playing outside in the grass as a tiny child, has never forgotten the love he has for this Earth.

The ring touched the stone. Jolted, startled, I watched as it sprang from my hand and fell to the chamber floor, breaking into two pieces. Unbidden, four words crashed into my mind.

'It is done, finished.' I turned and left.

Following the footpath back to the lane, I turned south and began making my way towards the A4080. I knew what I was looking for, and in a short while I found it. A public footpath sign guided me across a field, between the buildings of someone's home and then along the fringe of a small wood. I had practiced this skill so many times; my eyes swiftly assimilating the information they were receiving and calculating probabilities. I needed cover where I could lay up for the night and be confident of remaining undisturbed, a plentiful supply of sufficiently dry, dead wood and access to water. Within a few minutes I was setting up my camp and using the last of my birch bark to kindle my last fire. I found it hard to comprehend that my journey was over, and that in a few hours Joey would once more loom into my life; his beautiful and reassuring presence materialising as if from thin air.

With my back supported by a tree, I took all the time I needed to absorb this world that I was about to leave. My senses alert to every alien sound or signal of change, the shifts in wind and cloud-heralding weather changes, the moon's cycle, the temperature and the ever-changing fall and rise of hills and valleys. As I sat with a cup of tea, warming my amber-brown, woodsmoke-stained hands, two questions formed.

'What will I say to people? What do I bring back?'

And then, briefly, as I slid down and pulled the sleeping bag up to my chin,

'How do I stay alive with this journey?'

On neither account was there any need to be concerned. The seed had found the egg, and all that was needed was time.

I slept, lain on the leaf-strewn woodland floor, sleeping beneath the trees, a thousand yards from Bryn Celli Ddu, close by the Menai Straits on the Isle of Mona.

The chief leaned towards me.

'Until the day comes that the people of these islands remember their sacred duty to love and care for the Earth, the Children's Fire will remain extinguished. Until they remember that the thrushes, the rabbits, the trees and all waters also belong to and are loved by creation, there will be no justice. Until ceremonies are held honouring the seasons, and the youth is held by elders worthy of that name, there will be no lasting peace. Until this day comes, we will always be frightened of your people, for you see with dead eyes and your madness may be all it takes to tip the scales.'

She paused, and then, whispering: 'Mend what was broken. Rekindle the Children's Fire.'

JOURNEY LAND

Map 5

Chapter 5
The Far Shore

I HAVE KNOWN Joey for much, much longer than the seventeen
years since we both first heard each other's names and shook
hands. We have stood together in ceremony, danced to the same
tree, worked for the same vision and knelt before the same
wonders. When I saw his car, his familiar figure, his 'Joeyness',
I knew again the blessing of comradeship. Something else as
well – something that stretched back through mist, swamp and
forest. A sense of familiarity and recognition; a jolting nudge
that challenges everything my Western mind understands as real.
We have sat around fires together many times and the chain
of these fires stretches back along an invisible path of whose
beginning I have no knowledge. I cannot remember too much
about the car ride back to Devon, except that the seat was still
exquisitely comfortable, and Joey's presence a balm. The exotic
warmth of the car infused my body, mind and soul, holding me
weightless, suspended in space, and I surrendered fully. Upon
our arrival at Embercombe, I again entered the Inipi ceremony
lodge. Held in the dark heat of the Inipi, the glowing carmine
rocks, the plunge and hiss of water meeting fire, the rush of hot
steam and the canvas of images forming, lapsing and glowing,
I was emotional, tired and deeply content all at the same time.
Thankfulness rushed at me like the waves of a returning tide,

overwhelming and beyond words. When I eventually entered my home and put on the kettle, I was still hovering on the edge of re-entry, lapsing into prolonged periods of silent, unfocused staring and swiftly finding that, of necessity, I had to be outside, physically connected to nature. Emerging into the bright sunlit world of our valley my journey was *almost* complete, and it has remained this way ever since. Seven years later, I am still drinking from the same well and I do not expect it to change any time soon. Somewhere in the riven between-worlds that describes our relationship to time and place, I remain on the beach, looking out to sea and knowing that, one day, I will cross it.

We are a people walking home. We are searching the threads of a broken and forgotten story. It may be new, but in most respects I think it is the renewal of something that we once held close to our hearts and vivid in our imagination. Among other Amazonian indigenous tribes, the Achuar people speak of the Eagle and the Condor prophecy.

> The Eagle and the Condor is an ancient Amazon prophecy that speaks of human societies splitting into two paths – that of the Eagle, and that of the Condor. The path of the Condor is the path of the heart, of intuition and of the feminine. The path of the Eagle is the path of the mind, of the industrial and of the masculine.
>
> The prophecy says that the 1490s would begin a 500-year period during which the Eagle people would become so powerful that they would virtually drive the Condor people out of existence … The prophecy says that during the next 500-year period, beginning in 1990, the potential would arise for the Eagle and the Condor to come together, to fly in the same sky and to create a new level of consciousness for humanity. The prophecy only speaks of the potential…[38]

---

[38] Pachamama Alliance. https://blog.pachamama.org/the-eagle-and-the-condor-prophecy.

The prophecy speaks of 'potential' and advises us of the supreme honour our species has been given by creation. We get to choose. In ways that the cat sat on my lap will never know, we have to wrestle with choice. Elevated beyond the verifiable truth of our actions, my society claims to be rational. It would be funny if our actions were not so shockingly and disturbingly contrary to the evidence. We seem to apply our prodigious rational minds to almost everything, except and unless it threatens our short-term, material benefit. If these perceived material benefits are immense enough, we may extend the timeframe, but for rather more generous and inclusive aspirations, no matter their probity, we settle for turning the other way and procrastinating indefinitely. Whether carrying the teachings of the Bible, the Torah, the Qur'an, the Vedas, the Sutras, humanism or any other scripture or philosophy, the way we design our societies and live our lives tends to belie our lofty ideals. We abhor war, yet make millions manufacturing and selling weapons that will be used to make war. We hold the 'Golden Rule'[39] aloft, claiming our allegiance to the principle of treating others as we would ourselves be treated; yet, we vote in governments that slam the door on the opportunity to do so. Ignorance drives our behaviour and fear is the food upon which it is nourished. If I were the god of whose bewilderingly human attributes religion has tried to persuade me, I would be exasperated and disappointed beyond measure. I might even find myself tempted to uncharitable thoughts.

Walking across the border country from England to Wales, I crossed a line that once described the divide between the civilised world and the barbaric beyond. Of course, it was untrue; it was just a story that was promulgated for someone's benefit and, dancing to the same tune, sufficient numbers became complicit to give it power. So, millions died and millions were enslaved. In Gaul, Julius Caesar personally committed one million people

---

[39] Analects of Confucius 15:23, and versions found in every major wisdom tradition.

one way, and a further one million the other.[40] I think that a seed was sown in us around that time. A seed that later bore sour fruit, when we set about colonising the world. Abused, traumatised, culturally raped, spiritually castrated and with our Kanyini[41] broken, we began the unconscious road to hateful revenge – giving to the world what had been given to us. Even the same Roman justification was used; we set out to civilise the brute, soulless natives of benighted lands, awaiting our firm patrician guidance.

Born in 1949, just like the Romano-British story, I was raised to believe that our presence overseas was largely benign, mostly helpful – if also perhaps occasionally a little heavy-handed. Now married to a woman whose courage, generosity and open-heartedness have, and are, providing me with the happiest times of my life to date, and wishing to know something of her country's history, I made enquiry. My wife Wandia is Kenyan; her tribe, Kikuyu. It was the Kikuyu who revolted against British colonial rule in the 1950s, when I was a child, raised by loving parents who sought to instil their impressionable child with decent British values. In appreciation of George Monbiot's fulsome research and referencing,[42] I found my way to Caroline Elkins' book, *Britain's Gulag: The Brutal End of Empire in Kenya*. I thought I knew what brutal meant, but I have had to do some re-thinking.

> There were also local British officers whom the women knew by name ... [who] along with their minions perpetrated daily acts of brutality. They had no pity on those suffering around them. Rather than revolting these young British officers, the gruesomeness of their behaviour only aroused their eliminationist mentality. Or perhaps over time their repeated tortures and killing anesthetised them, wiping out any.

---

[40] Life of Caesar, XV:5; Life of Pompey, LXVII:10; also Pliny, VII:91ff.
[41] http://kanyini.org/tjilpi-bob-randall/.
[42] George Monbiot's website. www.monbiot.com.

Rape, castration, impalement, burning, starvation, flogging and monstrous methods of torture that sicken and repulse; this was the horrific truth of Britain's colonial strategy during the Mau Mau rebellion in Kenya. At the onset of the Mau Mau, and for a further three years, the British prime minister was Winston Churchill. It was not his finest hour.

To her enduring credit, Barbara Castle, the member of Parliament for Blackburn – yet to rise through the ranks of the Labour party to various high-ranking positions in government, including the honorific title of First Secretary of State – published this in 1955:

> In the heart of the British Empire there is a police state where the rule of law has broken down, where the murder and torture of Africans by Europeans goes unpunished and where the authorities pledged to enforce justice regularly connive at its violation.[43]

It seems that humanity has an almost unlimited capacity for both gross savagery and sublime kindness. It seems that this breadth of possibility is the calibrated scale upon which we have been challenged to score our mark on the universal story. From the primordial ocean of endless possibility, we have crossed a threshold and gained some measure of consciousness, a gift beyond imagination. It is through this window that we will see who we truly are, our radiant divinity and our corrosive depravity. It has already, and it will in future, cost us dearly. The price of knowing that we are invited to the Elysian Fields is only fully known when, crouched in the gullet of the toilet bowl, one hand reaches for the flushing lever in full knowledge that the choice sits with us.

What made it all the more shocking is that it was my father's generation who perpetrated this shameful episode in our history. The same generation who fought the Nazis, and pulled back

---

[43] Barbara Castle, 'Labour to find Kenya Thugs', *Tribune*, 30 September 1955.

in horror at the excesses of a regime wedded to the idea of racial superiority. Wandia's grandmother was still alive when we got married. I was a little apprehensive about how she might respond to the news that her granddaughter was marrying the son of those who so sadistically tortured and abused her people. In addition to this, I had unearthed another story that disturbed me greatly. My son's Kenyan family name is Kamau. Barbara Castle's courageous exposure of British atrocities in Kenya revealed the manner in which the life of one young man by the same name was tormented, abused, and broken.

He died, after several days of torture. Some money had gone missing in a police station where Kamau was employed. Suspecting Kamau, two British officers elected to obtain the truth. I don't know if my son is related to Kamau, but it is entirely possible. Missing two front teeth where a British soldier had smashed his rifle butt into her face, Wandia's grandmother had direct experience of our heavy-handedness. Close to 100 years old, she held Wandia's hand and said, 'It was a very long time ago' – but it wasn't really. Neither were the murderous events that took place in Visegrad in 1992, in Srebrenica in 1995, Beslan in 2004, Garissa in 2015 or the terrors afflicting Yemen right now, and in countless other places – many of which we know, even more that we will probably never hear about. When Eric Griffiths Jones, attorney-general in Kenya, drafted a memo to the colonial governor in 1957, he wrote:[44]

If we are going to sin, we must sin quietly.

The advice was heeded, the sinning indulged, the screaming muffled and the truth eventually exhumed.

***

---

[44] Ian Cobain and Richard Norton-Taylor, 'Sins of colonialists lay concealed for decades in secret archive', *Guardian*, 18 April 2012. www.theguardian.com/uk/2012/apr/18/sins-colonialists-concealed-secret-archive.

There was a point in my journey across Wales when I knew that, whatever barred my way, I would make it to Mona. There was a similar moment in my bigger life-journey when I knew that, whatever the shortcomings of my past and whatever the implications, this time I would honour the pledge I made under the night sky in the coastal mountains of northern California in 1984. The first time I took this pledge, it was only a few weeks after my return to the UK before I realised that I was already failing the spirit, if not the word, of a self-promise that had offered me everything for which my wild soul yearned. This was not because I had done anything that obviously contradicted the pledge, but rather that I simply had not done *anything*. I knew that I was passively enjoying the pretence of being committed to my pledge, while doing the bare minimum to sustain it. I could find a million reasons as to why the necessities of everyday life were more important than the expansive demand of my pledge's horizon. I knew that, deep within me, I was reluctant to inconvenience myself to the rigour of stepping outside the comfortable, predictable realm of my moderately interesting life. I knew that no one was watching and that, even if they were, my inaction would probably not be noticed. It might even be welcomed as further proof that we all ultimately submit to a quiet, comfortable and expedient life. I had to go through many thresholds before I reached a point of no return; real commitment does not come easy to me. On the other hand, once I get there, it takes a lot to dislodge me.

Early in our training, Tracker and I were given a task to achieve. It did not fit inside any preconceived notion of challenge that I had previously entertained because it was huge and beyond the scope of what I thought I was capable of. At a very disturbing and charged meeting, standing to attention and feeling that I was undergoing some kind of psychological waterboarding, I stood next to Tracker as our task was spelled out. We retired to our chilly tipi, tired and morose. I was appalled at the dimensions of this task, but Tracker seemed strangely at ease. A tense, and occasionally charged, conversation revealed that we both had very different interpretations of what had just transpired. I understood the task we had been given as non-negotiable and mandatory. Tracker understood it to be more on the lines of 'have a go'. Previous experience had taught me that things might not go well for us if we had no clarity. Our training was extremely demanding and we were permanently under the cosh of an unpredictable, irascible and acutely discerning teacher. Tense, and fearing the worst, we arranged a meeting, asked for clarity and had our worst fears confirmed as we were lambasted again. At this point, the UK Ambulance Service did not include crews trained to the specialist expertise of paramedics. We were given the task of changing this situation, and thereby saving the lives of many people in emergencies of one kind or another, who would benefit from the radically improved professional service. Since Tracker and I were only recently converted to the idea of 'going straight' and still coming to grips with the droll idea of living disciplined, purposeful lives, this seemed well beyond our reach. Clarity did not bring any relief, but at least we did not need to argue any more. Overwhelmed, and feeling doomed to failure, we clung to a straw that had been flung our way as we departed the meeting. Our teacher would introduce us to a military general in the British Army, who might, apparently, have some helpful ideas to contribute. I was not looking forward to meeting the general. It all felt rather hopeless and I feared we would not make a good first impression. As it happened we never did meet the general and, miraculously, a few years later, the UK introduced paramedics into its emergency services. Tracker and I may have briefly wondered if this was a result of our half-hearted pleas to an apparently indifferent creator, but it seemed unlikely. In any case, the only thing that really had our attention was the relief that we could now justifiably abandon this project and hope that the next would be more appropriate to our talents, aptitude and inexperience. There was one positive outcome from this sorry episode: my pride was wounded and I knew that, in order to achieve anything of significance, I needed to commit. I also needed to take the radical step of presupposing that I had gifts and potential far exceeding that which was currently visible to most others who knew me well; and to me.

Completing my journey to Mona, I felt as if I was full to bursting with information, experience and insight. I needed time to digest and assimilate. The years of mediated commitment were long past, so there were no self-doubting, internal voices to contend with. I just had to wait, remain attentive, listen and watch. Words spoken and quoted earlier in this book remained ever-present in my mind.

'Mend what was broken. Rekindle the Children's Fire.'

On the occasions that I used to dwell on the enormity of this task, I would shrink back, overcome by the disparity between the man that I am and the magnitude of the vision. The lens through which we perceive the world is all-important. Choosing rather to focus on the joy of committing my efforts to a world in which children are raised as creative, loving and courageous adults, who understand that their responsibility is 'to care for all living things', changes my outlook, lifts my spirits and engages the engine of purposeful action.

The further we travel away from Earth, physically and imaginatively, the more important it is that we hold the Earth close to our hearts. The 'Eagle and the Condor' legend speaks to the twin horizons of our essence as humans. As the eagle nations fly ever further into the jet stream of human potential in the external physical world, understanding the laws upon which our universe has been created, and manipulating energy to our advantage, we have unfolded one of the great wings defining our species. We are one part of the Earth dreaming herself alive. Correspondingly, the condor nation has continued its deep exploration of belonging to Earth, tending the garden, singing the songs of creation and dancing prayers of thankfulness and gratitude. Yet, in both cases they are much, much more than this. The Condor Nation has always probed the invisible, dreaming world of spirit; the sacred in plant, rock, river and forest. Theirs is an animate, conscious, raucously boisterous world, where time is understood cyclically, and membership of the Earth community is experienced moment by moment, heartbeat by heartbeat. They, too, have their science, and repeatedly throughout history they have understood and calculated mathematical equations that have astounded the eagle. Yet their centre, the totem around which they dance, is the revered mother from whose breast they have drawn milk and learned the practice of 'right-living'. The eagle is far more than the severe calculus of rational science. Where would the eagle's science be without imagination? The voyaging vision of many great female and male scientists has transported us to the miracle of creation, and not just insightful discoveries that have enabled the extraction of minerals ever deeper from the Earth's interior. Einstein is endlessly quoted for his acknowledgement and celebration of human attributes that go way beyond the banal importance of logic and rational process.

In this way, the head and tail of the great snake, Ouroboros, find each other, as the head swallows the tail and the circle becomes whole. It is a whole world we want, not one or the other, and this is the invitation of the 'Eagle and the Condor' prophecy. Whatever world we co-create over the coming decades, there will be no stopping bright minds asking questions that take us to the rim of knowledge and one step beyond, for this is part of who we are. Yet, several questions remain:

o   Shall we accept the invitation?
o   How do we bring the head to the tail?
o   What is my contribution?

I do not yet know our collective RSVP to this invitation. Judging by our actions to date, I would say that we seem predisposed to decline, but what the opinion polls indicate is not always how things work out. I have accepted the invitation and so have a great many others. I don't know how we bring the head to the tail, but one part of this great journey is remembering the indigenous soul that still lives in our eagle hearts, and reuniting the head and tail of our own British story. Only 2000 years ago, less than 0.25 % of the time that humans have walked on this tiny isthmus of land[45] and, much latterly, island, we still had a worldview that beheld the natural phenomena of nature with awe and reverence. As a tribal people connected to the long walk of our ancestors, a rich and textured culture that was far more refined and profound than historians taught us until a few years ago, we valued the Earth for what she is and has been forever. We may not have understood the mechanics of the miracle we beheld but, without equivocation, we acknowledged that it *was* a miracle. Gratitude and appreciation *were* expressed in our ceremonies, which were alive, vibrant and central to our identity as a people. The rivers, valleys and trees spoke to us, and we were familiar with the language. We did not feel lonely in the way that our orphaned future foretold; we belonged; we knew home; we were family. In my lifetime, we have taken a further step. We have removed our children from the embrace of the grandmothers, the great teachers. We have closed the door on nature, and it is badly hurting our children. The far shore names this as defilement, a gross injustice and a treaty broken. To do such a thing is to step about as far away from the Children's Fire as could possibly be conceived. As we reach out to the stars and find our way to abstractions that provide access to unimaginable powers, we must, we simply *must* rub our children with grass, smear them with mud, teach them to make fire and sleep in dens under the shifting skies of seasonal change. We must unlock the door to stories that will enable their humanity to remain bound to the soft tenderness of the summer seashore, and the aching raw bewilderment of the winter gale. They need this in the same way that they need water, food and shelter, the same way that they need physical proximity, touch and loving care.

We are not parented by humans alone; the forest is forever calling us home to its wild heart, and our bodies revel in knowing

---

[45] Rob Dinnis and Chris Stringer, *Britain: One million years of the human story* (London, National History Museum, 2014).

that we, too, were conceived in the colliding heat of sperm and egg. Our sexuality, so long banished to the netherworld of forbidden shadows and violent repression, will find peace in the loving arms of acceptance that the rest of nature enjoys and embraces. All parts of our humanity can be healed and gentled in the wisdom of the snake, Ouroboros – in welcoming, not denying the full reach of who we are and who we are called to be. When nature is welcomed back into religion, when we stop cutting off 'impure' bits from our babies and children,[46] when we twine refined intellect with emotional fluency and physical embodiment, when we allow the full recognition of sacredness in all aspects of life and living – then, then we will skim the voyage across the water to the far shore. In this way, the goddess takes her place alongside her male consort, and the condor flies with the eagle. Perhaps we even get to learn that raven's trick of flipping upside-down, so that, beneath and above the other, we mate in flight, tumbling in the blue sky, singing alive the creation story for ever and a day.

In June 2015, in the Black Hills of South Dakota and land sacred to the Great Sioux Nation, alongside 80 female and male dancers, I participated in my fourth sundance ceremony. This time, it was held by Loretta 'Afraid-of-Bear' Cook[47] and Tom Kanatakeniate Cook.[48] Loretta and Tom organise and hold this annual ceremony in accordance with the Lakota protocols set out in the seven sacred ceremonies handed down to the Lakota by White Buffalo Calf Woman. To those critical of allowing the participation of non-natives, they quote Chief American Horse, who said, 'Anyone may dance the sundance, if he will do as the Oglala do.' No fee was charged and no gift was requested; I was very privileged to be invited. I am neither Lakota nor belong

---

[46] Genital mutilation.

[47] Loretta 'Afraid-of-Bear' Cook is the faith-keeper and holder of the 'Afraid-of-Bear'/American Horse Sundance Pipe of the Oglala Lakota Nation.

[48] Tom Kanatakeniate Cook, Wolf Clan, Mohawk.

to any other Native American tribe; my roots are in Britain. I believe that the friendship and mentorship of my indigenous friends was extended to me because they recognised that I love our Mother Earth and am dedicated to doing all I can to speak the story of coming home, returning from exile and finding a seat at the table – not at the head of the table because, like my childhood's family dining table, it is circular, and in this form we can all see each other without craning our necks, and listen without diminishing ourselves. Evidence of how the people of a much younger Britain once possessed a worldview that embraced the full spectrum of a fecund cosmology, alive with relationships that joined together rather than held apart, grows year by year. Modern archaeology, wielding the tools of contemporary science and technology, in company with intuition, imagination and discernment, is providing access to our ancient past and toppling older interpretations shackled to the same feudal assumptions that endorsed the right to spread 'civilisation' around the world. Together with his frequent and endearing aspersions, cast in the direction of 'new age ideas' and proud declarations of 'lifelong atheism', I am a great admirer of the pre-historian Francis Pryor. In reading his book *Home*, I felt some of the warmth, intimacy and dignity of our ancestors – real people who lived real lives, which, for the most part, were concerned with food, shelter, tools and clothing; with friends, lovers, kith and kin. The small personal stuff that, thanks be, still fills our days, even now in the twenty-first century. All of the messy, textured minutiae of everyday life, yet also an infusion of sacredness that sees meaning and relationship in everything, inhabiting everything and extant everywhere. The invisible mystery of wonder that provokes the indrawn breath, the startled pause and the felt experience of beholding beauty.

> Excavations ... have shown that houses could also be shrines, and that religion and ritual played a hugely important part in providing structure to ordinary domestic life. I'm convinced that this fusion – this integration – of the sacred and the

domestic was a far more important feature of pre-historic and early historic home life than is generally recognised.[49]

Our roundhouses, our homes, used to face east or southeast towards the rising morning sun; our fires were in the centre of the roundhouse; the place opposite the door, against the wall, held special significance, and the internal microcosm of our homes seems to suggest a mirroring of the macrocosm – a worldview which, perhaps, entwined the eagle and condor. All of this is so similar to the tipi interior of the Lakota. During the period Pryor describes as the New Order,[50] 1500–1000 BCE, it seems that our ceremonies became less orientated around grand structures, like Stonehenge, and instead migrated home; becoming more local and integrated with everyday life. There is no evidence that this signalled a weakening of our animate worldview; it is just that we took it home with us, which was just as well, since we had fields and livestock for which to care. Water assumed greater importance in the rituals of this time, together with ceremonies that reflected the social standing and significance of women's role and place in society. An object that seems to cradle the unity we may once have known between the spiritual, the family, community and land is the quern-stone. Used to grind the family's corn, evidence abounds that suggests these stones were among one of the most valuable and treasured items of the time. Along with bowls, pots, weapons and jewellery, querns bridged different worlds and spoke of daily tasks imbued with spiritual significance and practical application. Even down to the habit of raiding the horses and cattle of neighbouring tribes, our ancestor's lives and concerns looked remarkably similar to the grandparents of those indigenous people who taught me. Why, with so much accumulating evidence, should we assume that we were any different? The passage below was written about the original Lakota. The author spent twenty-five years researching the culture, language, ceremonies and cosmology of

---

[49] Francis Pryor, *Home* (London, Penguin) p. 105.

[50] Pryor, *Home*, pp. 168–71.

this ancient people. She worked in collaboration with Chunksa Yuha, a Mdewakantonwan Dakota, born in 1905. Chunksa Yuha was raised speaking the archaic language of the old people, and kept out of schools, away from the white colonisers. He was one of eight children chosen by the elders to be taught and trained in the traditional ways, so that the old ceremonies and songs might be remembered. Chunksa Yuha was the only one of the eight still alive when he met Ruth Beebe Hill, a woman dedicated to telling the true story of a people that had once roamed free on its own land and in its own way. The resulting book was, and is, astonishing. Every word of her 2000-page manuscript was translated back into the archaic Dakota/Lakota, and then back into English, in order that her work would be authentic to the mind, consciousness and truth of the people about whom she wrote. It is entirely possible that these words might once have been written about us. My Native American friends believe so. I say that they may yet be written about us, and that it is towards this that we walk homeward-bound.

> His was the spirit not seeking truth but holding on to truth. And his was the mind nourished on choice. Whatever he needed to know, nature sooner or later revealed to him. And that which he desired to know – the best way to achieve his maximum spiritual potential – was the only mystery he chose to investigate.[51]

What was visited upon the indigenous tribes of north and south America, indeed upon almost all native peoples around the world, was nothing less than a catastrophe. With the stoic demeanour of the concerned bystander, perhaps we could relegate this horror story to the annals of history – hope to learn from the mistakes of our great-great-grandparents, if it were not for the fact that, shoved aside by successive governments and a disinterested electorate, the trauma continues to resonate. In

---

[51] Ruth Beebe Hill, *Hanta Yo* (New York, Double Day & Co, 1979), Foreword.

'God's own land', the USA, and in Canada, the descendants of a proud and dignified people experience catastrophe as a daily reality, even now. Unlike Britain, on this continent the 'Romans' never physically left and the virus continues to spread and ravage. Studying the experience of indigenous people in North America we see how entire nations can be culturally, socially, economically and spiritually brought to their knees, enslaved to an alien culture that has no interest in their rehabilitation, only wishing that they would step aside and stop spoiling the view. In an article in the *Washington Post*, Sari Horwitz quotes Theresa Pouley, the chief judge of the Tulalip Tribal Court in Washington state, and a member of the Indian Law and Order Commission.

> One-quarter of Indian children live in poverty, versus 13% in the United States. They graduate high school at a rate 17% lower than the national average. Their substance-abuse rates are higher. They're twice as likely as any other race to die before the age of 24. They have a 2.3% higher rate of exposure to trauma. They have two times the rate of abuse and neglect. Their experience with post-traumatic stress disorder rivals the rates of returning veterans from Afghanistan.[52]

It is the children who suffer most. When I arrived in the Black Hills for the sundance last year, I met some of them. Beautiful, sensitive, intelligent and very fine young human beings, these girls had tried to kill themselves only a few days previously. It is heartbreaking to see such things close-up. The prisoner and the gaoler both live in the same pathology; neither is free. The terrifying excesses of human hatred towards any 'other', towards nature and even towards our own children, only takes hold when we try to turn away from the long shadow of our history. Written in invisible ink on the pages of this history is the stark observation that if our species is to steer a path towards peaceful

---

[52] Sari Horwitz, 'The Hard Lives – and suicide rate – of Native American children on reservations', *Washington Post*, 9 March 2014.

co-existence with ourselves and with all life, we must attend to the aftermath of trauma – the pervasive despair that, left to itself, will corrupt and eventually unravel the chance of future generations to live happy, purposeful lives. The vast majority of young people in Britain do not suffer as their indigenous sisters and brothers do in North America and around the world, but we would be mistaken to believe that we are forever safe. Supporting corrupt and brutal regimes; selling arms to whoever can afford them; choosing profit, power and self-interest over basic human rights and social justice; marginalising the disadvantaged and turning a blind eye to the misery of people with no home, no protection and no future. All these suggest that our shadow is alive and well, barely contained and biding its time. Trauma is deep in our DNA and at least one of the worms of this writhing discomfort found a home in our collective psyche two millennia ago.

Human beings, including all indigenous peoples, have always demonstrated a tendency towards behaviour unworthy of the privileges that evolution has provided us, but the likelihood of a peaceful, sustainable future will be greatly enhanced if we politely decline the invitation to:

> Be fruitful and multiply and fill the earth and subdue it, and have dominion over the fish of the sea and over the birds of the heavens and over every living thing that moves on the earth.[53]

In 1455 and 1493, the Vatican issued two papal bulls. They were proclaimed as a mandate from the 'one true God' and his son, Jesus Christ. The first of these edicts set out an objective, or more accurately a responsibility, that has authorised wholesale genocide, theft, slavery and violence against indigenous people ever since.

---

[53] *The Bible*, Genesis 1:28, English Standard Version.

[T]o invade, search out, capture, vanquish and subdue all Saracens and pagans whatsoever, and other enemies of Christ wheresoever placed, and the kingdoms, dukedoms, principalities, dominions, possessions, and all movable and immovable goods whatsoever held and possessed by them and to reduce their persons to perpetual slavery, and to apply and appropriate to himself and his successors the kingdoms, dukedoms, counties, principalities, dominions, possessions and goods, and to convert them to His and their use and profit.[54]

At the time of writing, this command is still valid and extant. It is neither rescinded nor publicly regretted, and in some places it is still used to justify actions that transgress international law on human rights and social justice. For more than 500 years it has broken faith with the Golden Rule. In the northern hemisphere this spring, as wild flowers answered the call of sunlight and warmth, offering millions of tiny benedictions to the delight of countless humans, indigenous elders from around the world gathered in Rome. A delegation of these elders sought an audience with Pope Francis I, asking him to revoke the edicts, and together with them announce to the world community that, irrespective of age or gender, all humans have the right and freedom to worship at the altar of their choice and not be judged less if their beliefs and practices differ from others.

I have no doubt that, in time, these papal bulls will be revoked and, by virtue of this single and yet hugely significant action, the 'eagle and the condor' will reduce the distance that separates one wingtip from the other. The indigenous elders gathering in Rome is a beginning, and if it accomplishes its goal, perhaps it will signal a new era in which we can acknowledge the gross injustices of the past, honour broken agreements and learn to live together more harmoniously. The manner in which we have treated the original peoples of the Earth corresponds to the

---

[54] Pope Nicholas VI, Romanus Pontiflex – Papal Bull, 1455.

way we have treated the Earth herself. This is still reflected in negative and exploitative attitudes to women – attitudes that are essentially repressive and violent. The same mind-set underwrites the rush to globalisation, and the corporatisation of everything that can be capitalised, against which a financial value can be ascribed. If we cannot find the courage to confront and resolve our species' dysfunctional relationship to the Earth's abundant generosity, then the future does not bode well for the universe. As we totter into space, growing in confidence and exporting the same value-set, we will inevitably enact the same ignorant story so starkly set out in the papal bulls of the fifteenth century. With this in mind, the 'long march' to Rome and the rescinding of the papal bulls is comparable to unlocking a gate on a pilgrimage pathway that could potentially allow the whole of humanity to engage a conversation about healing and reconciliation. It could be a stepping-stone to questions that challenge our unconscious assumptions about civilisation and the pursuit of happiness. It could lead to a wholesale shift in the entire trajectory of the human story that might leave even the most visionary of science-fiction writers open-mouthed with disbelief. Even now, we can gentle the suspicious and wary ape, which so fearfully and bravely ventured out of the forest onto the vast savannah.

The piece that we need, however, is the piece upon which we have been most terribly betrayed. We have to rediscover the numinous, the sacred and the divine, uncluttered and uncompromised by human institutions that have dubious intentions and flawed ethics. Every cell in our bodies yearns for the homecoming. Whatever the horrors religion has inflicted upon the world, it has also been the means by which countless millions have been encouraged and inspired to find and give the best of themselves. The form in which we currently accommodate this innate, instinctual response to the awe and wonder revealed by our consciousness needs to change, and we find this difficult. It raises the full panoply of primitive defence mechanisms that have enabled our survival over millennia. We will not relinquish them easily. Fortunately, tenacity is a proven and confirmed human asset. In my bones, I think we can do this. All parts of the emerging new story are about integration, collaboration, inclusion and wholeness. In the same way that our earliest spiritual and religious ceremonies embraced the mysterious, primordial splendour of the vast unknown territory that lay beyond the horizon, the birth of our babies, the seasons and the tides, we, too, need to reclaim eyes that can truly see what is spread before us. We have to bring all of nature to our altars, and acknowledge the sacred in ordinary, everyday living. We have to bring it home to where it belongs, with families, community, food-growing and then on, out into the broad territories of work, education, commerce, art, science and technology. We are being asked to imagine ourselves anew, to accept and grow our talents without collapsing into the arms of hubris. We are invited to come home to what we love; to develop and deploy our gifts; be mindful of our responsibilities and in continuous, exploratory dialogue, move to action.

What are the alternatives? There are many, I expect, but the favourite appears to be to push on regardless. To ignore what is obvious and just keep talking about economic growth, celebrity, shopping, credit card debt, the lottery and a few miserable weeks of a holiday spent in an artificially constructed paradise, only to be vomited back into the workplace (or not) on Monday, there to remain until the following year. Calgacus, a warrior chief of the Caledonian, supposedly spoke these words on the eve of the battle of Mons Graupius in 84–83 CE:

> Robbers of the world, having by their universal plunder exhausted the land, they rifle the deep [seas]. If the enemy be rich, they are rapacious; if he be poor, they lust for dominion; neither the east nor the west has been able to satisfy them. Alone among men they covet with equal eagerness poverty and riches. To robbery, slaughter, plunder, they give the lying

name of civilisation ... When they have made the world a desolation they call it Peace. [55]

Whether actually spoken by Calgacus or fabricated by Tacitus, these same words could easily have been voiced by an indigenous spokesperson of the twenty-first century. In the uncompromising language of a people that has suffered and expects to suffer more, this small fragment of text perhaps also speaks to the political and economic ambitions of several contemporary world powers. After several thousands of years of the same story, it is time for a change.

We still dream, and rightly so. Deep inside the soul of every human, we know that the far shore beckons. With only a very few exceptions, I found the latter-day Dobunni, Silures, Ordovices and Gangani to be generous, hospitable and fun. On the far shore is the possibility, entirely within our reach, of a human family that has chosen to commit to the kind, generous, peaceful, compassionate and loving teachings that have always been located in the heart of every true wisdom tradition and authentic religious teaching. Were we simply to act in accordance with our words, the gulf would close and the Selkies[56] might safely guide us through the waves, to shore. With some relief, I prefer to, again, return to the Kogi Indians' understanding of our purpose on this Earth, 'To care for all living things'; or the indigenous people who first declared the law of the Children's Fire; or the Golden Rule, ubiquitous to many world religions. We are bound to nature, exist as part of nature, find healing in nature and force a separation at our peril. Our past is with nature and so is our future. Growing up sufficiently to admit this single and gentle truth will bring us to right relationship with life. From here, we can contemplate the pathway to wisdom and take the next baby steps.

***

---

[55] Tacitus, *Agricola*, XXX.
[56] Mythological sea(l) creatures found in Scottish and Irish folklore.

Almost one year after my long walk I retraced my steps, searching for, and finding, all but two of my campfires. This time, I travelled by car. It was nothing like as cold as the previous winter and the world looked very different from the warm car interior. Nonetheless, parking and walking sections of the route, I found myself, on many occasions, transported back in time. Even though I had the support of satellite-assisted grid references to trace my invisible footprints, many miles of countryside often separated them and some of these stretches looked persistently unfamiliar. On the charred remains that marked the locations of the fires that had cooked my food, lightened my heart and boiled water, I practised the ancient skill that set us apart from our animal relations: I turned 'dead' wood into flame using a bow-drill. I sat beside each tiny new fire and felt into the space between now and then. I lay down on the earth with my head next to some of these fires and, by one of them, I slept. At each camp I offered my thanks and gratitude for the rest, comfort and safety I had found at each nested home. On more than one occasion, I wept. At several of these places I found my woodpiles still neatly stacked, just as I had left them twelve months previously. I found my senses to be acutely tuned to the evocative presence of the same trees, birds and scent of the land. I think I grieved for the even deeper sense of presence that I had felt when, exhausted and aching, I sat in a world of ice, snow and frozen stillness, listening to the owls and the subtle footfall of animals, unseen in the dark world surrounding my haven. I watched the moon wane and wax and, precisely positioned on one of my early fires outside Hereford, I found the complete skeleton of a rabbit laid across the blackened hearth. I wondered if, dying, it had chanced upon the warm embers and laid down to sleep the long sleep. I have often wondered about that rabbit.

I had another reason for returning along the trail of my journey. I wanted to try and find the people who had so generously befriended me, and thank them. I found myself wandering through small towns and villages like Pembridge, Knighton, Presteigne, Machynlleth and Beddgelert, stopping at service stations and peering into coffee bars. I knocked on doors, climbed gates, made phone calls and found quite a few of the people I sought. In most cases they were embarrassed to be thanked for what had felt like very small kindnesses. I realised that, in general, we have very little understanding of the impact we have on the people around us. I probably discomfited them even further, as I tried to describe their contribution to my wellbeing on those frigid arctic days and nights; as I felt into the world of long-departed ancestors and the prayers they sank beneath the waters of springs, lakes, rivers and seas. I attempted to voice the ache in my heart that comes from having my land named soulless. Although they did not know it, I passed on a message from the ravens, for I was, and I am, irredeemably lost to a world that exists as life itself exists, but whose image has faded, like old cloth, and is no longer seen.

> You, who believe yourselves separate, you must wake up soon. The sunrises and sunsets, the feasts and famines, the blazing story of becoming and departing, deserves rather more than your casual indifference. You are both the sorcerer and the bewitched. Trapped inside a spell of your own making you have only to open one eye. That's what Odin was trying to teach you. Wake up, wake up, this is too good to miss. Your wild cousins still ride the breath that you call wind. We are still here and we still remember. Wake up, do we have your attention? Yes, you're very clever. Well done. Hurrah. Can we move on? Now then, where were we?

In one year from the time of writing, I will be seventy. During the last eighteen months I have been variously diagnosed as having had a stroke, a brain tumour and a small brain abnormality that I have probably had since birth. Currently, it seems that the first two of these were misdiagnoses, which is just as well, since the third option is significantly less threatening to my wellbeing and future prospects. The gift of this erratic pathway has been to further deepen my determination to live – while I am alive and have the means so to do. This is the raw, blunt and unambiguous option we so often orbit and so rarely penetrate. Hedged in by insurance policies, legislation, career advice and the small, fast-food dreams that have infiltrated the immense vistas laid out before us, we choose instead the low road. The far shore cannot be attained without risk, or with certainty. Sooner or later, we have to plunge into the sea and strike out for a braver future. Beneath snatched breaths and plunging limbs, the monsters of the deep will stir and shift to wakefulness, slowly rising from the depths to keep appointment with destiny. The spectre of their malefic intent only grows if we wish them away. We have always loathed that which remains in the subterranean world of our dark unconscious. Yielding to loneliness, we may cry out into the darkness and be tempted to head back to the beach, where our discarded clothes lay crumpled and cold, as the moist air crackles and tiny shards of ice encrust with frost that which was once familiar. At such times, we hope. We hope for a passing ship, a ray of golden light and a voice whispering kind advice; an upsurge of strength. The beast from the deep draws close, and panic takes us in her arms. The death we so greatly fear comes close and into those dark eyes we stare until, looking again, we see her as she truly is: the dolphin offering us its broad back and a safe passage to the distant, churning shore. Those eyes, once fancied as soulless, nightmare chasms of abandonment, unimagined dimensions of cruelty, sorrow grieving for what might have been; those eyes, reflecting back what lives in us; nothing to do with the monster. Nothing to do with the force of nature we call dolphin, or tree, or flower, or wolf, or moon – just life calling us home. We hope for a lantern swinging in the darkness, a strong arm reaching down and lifting us to safety. We hope for all kinds of miracles and, sometimes, as the stars align and synchronicity responds, they happen. The dolphin, emissary of life, messenger of a deeper wisdom and eager to infiltrate our determined egotism, eases us into the shallows as we stagger to shore, where new clothes await, folded, warm and soft. The cresting waves tumble, and phosphorescence wreathes us in stars of sparkling silver. Now a dark streak heading back out to sea, leaping the rolling waves that forever beat upon our shore, the dolphin half-turns and smiles a blessing.

The politicians and soldiers of ancient Rome who smashed the ribcage of trees that guarded our sacred ceremonies, who dipped scarred hands inside the soft-petalled centre of our dreaming prayers and tore the still-pulsing heart from its fractured lodging, were one dislocated part of our human story. Rome lives in me, as it does in you, and it certainly lives in the hateful resurgence of all movements that tell a story of separation, blame, supremacy, control and violence. All it takes is our weak connivance, unwillingness to question and passive acquiescence. As with the story enacted between races, religions, countries and empires, so it is within us.

Although I empathise with Francis Pryor when he concedes in *Home* to regarding the Romans in Britain with some degree of aversion,[57] the image I see in the mirror tells me that Rome is alive and well in my only partially mapped interior. Our great task is to step beyond right and wrong, good and bad, and pledge ourselves to integration. Endlessly stressing the light and attempting to banish the dark only forces it into exile and it is here that, invisible to our facile idealism, it grows in strength and power, to quietly manipulate. It has not served us well to believe our ancestors to be stupid, brutish and ignorant. This is the story that all invaders, conquering forces and conceited ideologies have attempted to embed in the mind and memory of the people they wished to enslave. When I walked across this land, this small part of Earth from which I was born, I became a few steps more intimate with my grandparents, my storyline, myself and my heart. I threw off one more chain-link and, in the winter of 2009, heard again the ancient, wild chorus of freedom that our tribal people once hurled into the vast beyond. I am indigenous to the Earth, to this land. My heart is wild and, in the company of my wild animal, plant and rock relatives, I feel safe

---

[57] Pryor, *Home*, p. 275.

and close to spirit. However, everything beautiful and sacred lives in people as well, and I am moved beyond words by our own species. If we can only commit to confronting atrocity wherever it exists, attending to the healing of victim and perpetrator alike, aligning religion with nature, designing our societies to principles that guide us towards love and compassion, and binding our cleverness to the deeper aspiration of wisdom, perhaps we will indeed make it to the far shore.

There are layers to this word 'hope'. Without hope, we are walking towards death; for contained in this small word is our reason for living, the meaning that makes sense of all endeavour, the successes and the failures. Hope holds on to the belief that one day things might get better, even if this 'one day' is too late for us. After all, we can always hand it on to those following. When hope is extinguished, many give up and die. By far the most common experience of hope, however, is much more flaccid and limp than this. Everyday hope buys a lottery ticket or, if particularly inspired, several. This kind of hope never seems to get as far as taking responsibility for those whom we say we love. It never entertains the possibility of collusion with apathy. Nonetheless, even this parody of real hope, this ridiculously confident expectation of miraculous salvation sometimes induces startling results; such is the goodwill woven into life's design. One incident in particular burnt this realisation on to my feeble understanding of this profound notion of hope. Together with my woman-friend of the time, I was driving through the Black Forest in Germany. It was late and nightfall was imminent. Some questionable map-reading had brought us down lanes that seemed to shrink in girth, threatening to crush us between the two verges. On either side was a ditch from which, once in, the car would not be able to be extricated. Needing to turn around and head back the way we had come, another poor decision resulted in me frantically spinning the steering wheel as I attempted a thirteen-point turn on a road that was not much wider than the car was long. By force of will we almost made it, but not quite. In the final manoeuvre, I dropped one of the rear wheels into the ditch and the car, no doubt exhausted and dispirited, slumped down on to its chassis and refused to go further. Struggling to hold back the inevitable likelihood that we would probably have to remain in the car overnight, walk many miles and be caused great expense, my friend and I discussed the vague hope that someone might chance upon us and feel disposed to help. Given that the landscape around us looked much as it might have done a few millennia past, the impending darkness and no sign of human habitation made us feel no better. With hope teetering on the edge of a glass half-empty we waited, and around the fringe of the forest came a small group of men. They were huge – in fact, probably the biggest people I have ever seen in my life. Not fat, just massive. Surveying our predicament and scarcely uttering a word, they motioned to us to withdraw, and then taking up position at the car's rear, they made several herculean efforts to lift the car back on to the road. It was a prodigious effort; awe-inspiring, intimidating, but ultimately unsuccessful. I was mouthing what I hoped were soothing German phrases, expressing a subtle blend of gratitude and commiseration, when I began to see that, far from admitting defeat, they seemed to be reluctantly accepting that a more radical option was required. Confused and a little anxious, I kept hearing the word 'Mütter'. Abruptly, one of the giants left the group and made for a farmhouse that, until that moment, I hadn't seen, as it was almost completely screened by the forest. A long silence ensued until the man returned, evidently relieved and once again speaking of Mütter. The remainder of this tale is cloaked in the half-remembered images of radical bewilderment. Emerging from the forest came a woman of vast proportion. Whatever scale I had been operating on before was dismissed as irrelevant. The giant sons became large, but in no sense was their size comparable to the impatient colossus that advanced upon my car. She clearly thought that her sons had failed her expectations and that they had interrupted her during some household task; she made clear her intention to swiftly accomplish this minor undertaking before getting back to whatever it was that she was doing before. With curt and absolute authority, she commanded the men into various positions around the rim of the car before straddling the ditch and placing herself at the key position. Massive hands grasped the car and, after checking her sons' readiness, she bellowed a stentorian 'Eins, zwei, drei!' before flexing and deploying the full power of her phenomenal strength. Together with her sons, she lifted our car back on to the road. Hope can turn up trumps, but at this level it cannot be relied upon; in any case, it is usually an abdication of responsibility.

Between the flabbiness of lame hope, and the hope without which the universe would implode and all worlds collapse, sits the field of which Rumi spoke. It is here that we should meet. This small meadow is beyond the selfish preoccupations of tired stories that make it all seem as if we have no say in anything; as if we are all pawns sacrificed to the cruel indulgencies of gods who pass the time of day in much the same way as those British officers who abused Kamau. This is the council ground of the Children's Fire. It is beyond the infantile hope of salvation or the coming of a saviour. It places the future of this most beautiful world, all beings, all life, in our hands and says, 'choose life'. As the prophet said,

> By their *works* you shall know them.[58]

On 30 January 2010, one year after I had completed my 2009 journey and on the last day of the return trip during which I had searched for and revisited the charred remains of each night fire, I crossed the bridge to Mona. This was the final moment of my ceremony, when everything was complete and all had been done, as it should be. At the furthest point of my journey, in the place where I had looked out to the Celtic Sea and felt the grey wind of the netherworld tug at my elder memory, I

---

[58] *World English Bible*, Matthew 7:16.

stood again. Ceremonies have layers and, given a subtle blend of space and attention, they will speak to us over many cycles of moon and sun. Addressed directly, and with the penetrating, unblinking gaze of the raptor, they seem to shy away, preferring the splash of brief glimpses seized at the unfocused periphery. I was present with the sea; present with the understanding that these waves had never once ceased or paused since I last stood with the water lapping at my boots thirteen months previously, and for millions of years before then. I turned and walked away from the sea, feeling the sand crunch and grind beneath my feet. As I came to the first tufts of Marram Grass, something caught my eye. I looked up and there, tied to a stick buried vertically into the sand, was a bunch of flowers still wrapped in cellophane, the price clearly visible on the wrapping. I was startled. In symphony with the unknown soul who had done exactly the same thing two years previously, and laid a bunch of flowers on the flanks of the ancient British Camp where I had begun my journey, these flowers spoke the language of love and loss. Everything that had risen before and within me corkscrewed into my soft interior and I knelt on the sand, grieving the broken story of a people I still love, joyous to be alive and capable of feeling. Deeply happy that I am given to the rivers, to the trees, to the skies and to the forest, and that I, with others, am returning to join my family, the ceremony ground of true belonging.

77 CE, the Isle of Mona

A seagoing curagh is brought alongside a small landing platform on the north coast as two women, two men and an eight-year-old girl board the vessel. Taking her seat by one of the women, the girl reaches for the hand of a tall figure standing on the rocks waiting to bid them farewell. The tide is turning and the ship's master glances uneasily out to sea.

'Time to dip our oars and hoist sail, mistress.' The voice is gruff, anxious. Taking the child's hand in both of hers, the woman crouches and speaks the blessing of Mona. A moment of time that stretches between what is and what could have been; red tears splashing on the fractured bones of dreams that once held hope. Silence intervenes and the boat slides down a retreating wave, turning for Hibernia. Unheard, yet seen and felt, the words 'I love you' skim the waves and find home. All eyes turn to the horizon.

Two hours later, the master of the ship furls the sail as a brief ceremony takes place. An object wrapped in hide, bound with cords and decorated with wild flowers is released to the surging depths. A song curls around the bobbing craft and memories are bound together with dreams, held in the ocean waters until a new era when what was lost may be found again; the snake finds its tail, the eagle flies with the condor, people of all faiths and no faith join hands and, lifting their heads high, offer their voices of aching joy and indebtedness to the delicate mystery of life on Earth.

The ceremony complete, the sail is again hoisted and the looming landmass of Hibernia draws closer.

Chapter 6
Rekindling the Children's Fire

A WAXING CRESCENT moon and the vernal equinox. Light, liquid amber flows across the land as darkness gracefully yields to the choreography of the planetary dance. More snow is forecasted but it is unlikely to be with us for long. The blackbirds are already nesting and everywhere there is a quickening, a sloughing-off of wintery ways in salute to the sun as it strides higher in the sky and flamboyantly flings the promise of new life out into the solar system and beyond. Last night, my fourteen-month-old son, Cai, picked something up from the living room floor, swallowed it and choked. He cried out in terror and pain as he fought to dislodge the object by vomiting, retching and convulsing. The incident probably lasted no longer than two minutes, but it was very frightening for Cai, his mother and me. I held him upside down, slapping his back, but whatever it was remained stuck fast. We were on the verge of dialling 999 when I sensed a slight shift in his cries. Wandia thrust a finger into his mouth and withdrew a regurgitated flexible plastic ring about one inch in diameter. A short while later, Cai was intermittently nuzzling his mother's breast and happily playing with one of his toy animal companions, a rather overstuffed dog upon whom he lavishes multitudes of very wet, open-mouthed kisses, random admonishments and hooting barks that he has perfected from careful observation of neighbouring dogs. His parents, meanwhile, were still struggling with the aftershock of his most recent mishap and reeling from the shocking awareness such incidents invoke; the realisation that the abyss is never far away. We understand things like this. It is immediate and there is no equivocation. In this kind of situation many people show great courage, humanity and kindness. Beyond this, however, we struggle with the abstract calamities that lazily unfurl. All around us, thousands of species walk quietly towards extinction, the temperatures of polar regions softly climb higher, and power continues its stealthy glissade into the open, moist palms of the world's smallest private club. In the timeline of Earth's history, the descent into human-created environmental crisis has been sudden and dramatic. To the perpetrators, excepting a tiny minority, the crisis has only recently been even acknowledged and still our actions lag a long way behind the rhetoric. This collective failure to appreciate the swiftness and magnitude of these developments presents us with grave challenges. Only half-awake, we are unlikely to act and, even if we do, to what end will our actions be directed? My child, my family, my money, my food, my water... or ours, and what is the circumference that describes 'ours'? How far does it extend? I understand the entire course of my winter journey to Mona as being an exploration of these questions, an exploration of the nature, meaning and implications of loving. I can only truly love that with which I am intimate and it is my observation that many of us are the same in this. If we are to come together, join hands and resolve some of the mess that we have made, we will have to open our hearts to a far deeper and more expansive experience of love than hitherto we have considered possible – or even desirable. This is the teaching of the Children's Fire.

Some pages previously, we hovered unseen above a circle of chiefs who sat in council around the Children's Fire on unidentified wild land of great beauty a couple of hundred years ago. Perhaps we marvelled at the simplicity, pragmatism and complexity of the pledge that the chiefs had made. Perhaps our imagination was able to conjure the very spot where they sat, the small stand of trees, the far-sighted view over the valley, the scents and smells, the sounds particular to place and season. Then the involuntary gesture of dismay; the sharp indrawn breath; the disbelief and disappointment as the circle foundered on rocks strewn in its path by a cultural mind that has no capacity for empathy. Everything exists at a point somewhere on the wheel of renewal and decline. Even our lives are only most richly treasured by the knowledge that in time we will die. The choices a person makes that prompt others to describe them with admiration or disapproval always leaves open the question of the future. The trail behind is not proof of the trail ahead. It is a principle of nature and in this I find both anxiety and some comfort. Strewn amongst the buried archaeology of our story here in the British Isles, the dreaming of a people who once knew and understood sacredness as it applies to things we now consider valueless still wreathes and curls, whispering seditious heresies that may yet save the day. Even as we have triumphed we have also declined; sublime achievements are twinned with a grotesque betrayal of trust, to each other, to all that is more than human and, of course, to the young and unborn of all species.

The fire that had held the chiefs close to their pledge was maintained by their spiritual presence, intellectual acuity, emotional honesty and commitment to courageous action. When this failed, when their Kanyini was broken, the council became fractured. The original peoples of all lands have at some time or other encountered the venal power that eventually evolved into our common idea of civilisation and they have never recovered. The grandparents of the people who taught me lived during a prolonged physical and cultural genocide, and it still reverberates. Our chiefs, our grandparents, those that later perpetrated the same atrocities, suffered the same trauma, and it still reverberates. So deeply embedded are the unconscious cultural assumptions and beliefs interred in the way we now live that we are almost incapable of seeing the nihilism that squats at the centre. A god if ever there was a god. At the ever-extending alpha of human ingenuity and the ever-deepening omega of disconnection, loneliness and hubris, the irony is that perhaps there has never been a better chance of rekindling the Children's Fire than now. For this to be the case we need to awaken to the invidious story that has held us enslaved for so very long, allow the fire to thaw our frozen-feeling nature and come alive to who we truly are. In this we can make the choice that will explode the myth of our innate egotism and selfishness, opening an infinitely more exciting chapter in our journey towards wholeness.

Let us imagine that we were all once chiefs in the council circles that radiated around the Children's Fire and, if it's not too painful, that we were all in some way culpable for allowing the fire to become untended. Let us imagine that even now we are only half-awake to the soul intention that brought us out of the forests and into the savannahs all those millennia ago. Let us imagine that the dreaming of our ancestors, moving and touching us in moments of unguarded receptivity, is just another way of listening to ourselves talking in our sleep. Let us imagine that after a period of amnesia and confusion we are now beginning to orientate ourselves to the pulse of the drummer who calls us back to the council circle to reclaim our seat at the council of chiefs. Let us imagine that sat upon the earth, head down, we slowly lift our gaze to the heart-breaking, heart-making joy of knowing that the Children's Fire once again lights our way. Be still. Listen. You may just hear the snap, crackle and pop of the first twigs catching. Tiny flames dancing, swirling, twisting and reaching, like a cave painting reflected onto your glistening, beseeching eyes. Lean forward and, with outstretched arms, cup the flames in your hands and thrust the fire deep inside your belly. Now she burns inside you and everything is changed, forever.

There is a ceremony that awaits your attention. It is the answer to an invitation. In order to qualify as fit to perform this ceremony you need to be willing to live by your promises, or at least, and perhaps more realistically, to live by *this* promise, as a start. The invitation provided to you by all that is beautiful on this, our Earth, is that you become a council chief by pledging allegiance to the Children's Fire.

> 'No law, no decision, no commitment, no action, nothing of any kind will be permitted to go forth from this council of chiefs that will harm the children.'

The catch is that this pledge is only the beginning. To live by the promise of the Children's Fire you will be required to walk as a peacemaker, whilst forever stepping towards the most radical, profound, honest and courageous version of yourself that is possible in the time that you have alive. For this reason alone it is best not to rush, but rather to take your time, reflect, ask questions and prepare. I suspect that there are many who will refuse the invitation simply because to accept it flies in the face of everything we have learned and been brought up to believe, even when in our hearts the answer is a quiet and resolute 'Yes, I accept'. In many ways we have become institutionalised and twisted out of shape. There are few things that we can do more helpful to our wellbeing than to surprise ourselves by doing something out of character that extends the person we have come to believe ourselves to be. So, to those who might feel foolish doing such a thing I say: do it privately, unseen, but do it. The pledge of the Children's Fire, like so much of the wisdom handed down to us from indigenous people, is an insightful blend of the spiritual and the pragmatic. The Children's Fire is nothing if it isn't also common sense.

Preparing for the ceremony is important. If, in our eagerness, we rush to the assignation that we understand to be the 'important' bit, we lose the opportunity to build intention and potency. It is a subtle process. Move too quickly and there is no power because we have moved ahead of ourselves and, unlike the skilled tracker, we have committed to the next step before we know upon what it is our foot will rest. Move too slowly and eventually our progress will become hesitant, vague and unfocused. Continue to move too slowly and it will never happen. We are required to search and discover the subtle interplay between disciplined intention and receptive intuition.

o   Learn how to make an outside fire using twigs and sticks that you have gathered. If such skills are already yours, take it deeper and experiment. Wherever your starting point is, move into a place where you have to apply yourself and properly attend.

o   Discover a place where you can safely, and without injury to the environment, have a *small* fire in solitude. Choose this place or be guided to this place by virtue of the same unity of spiritual intention and practical consideration. Ask permission of the land, trees and creatures who live in this place to hold your ceremony.

o   Gather three or four handfuls of twigs and sticks and take them home with you. Tie them into a bundle and place them somewhere significant and respectful in your home. Occasionally take your bundle and sit holding it in your arms, feeling into the ceremony, feeling into your pledge, feeling into the implications. Never treat the bundle of sticks casually or betray their significance by referring to them in terms that make you feel dishonest or ashamed. You have gathered a bundle of ancient sunlight masquerading as a bundle of dead sticks. The energy in your bundle is colossal. It only awaits combustion.

o   At a time of your choosing, carry your bundle of sticks to the place where they will be lit. Do not invite others to join you unless you are sure that they will fully and unreservedly support you with their goodwill and respect. Light your bundle using whatever method you have practised and, once it is fully alight, pulsing and leaping for the sky, make your pledge aloud. If need be, say it as many times as it takes to feel that it has indeed been spoken. Then take your time and sit with the echo. Allow yourself to feel good. You have a seat at the council as a chief. You have taken the pledge of the Children's Fire. You are changed forever; something has been planted, and in time it will grow and yield fruit.

o Ensure that the fire is properly doused and that your ceremony is closed in a manner that is respectful and responsible. Give thanks and offer your gratitude. Leave some small gift of food for the families of other beings living close by, that none go hungry this day.

If, in your unique situation, finding sticks, making a bundle and lighting it is not possible, then substitute a candle. In this case also, take your time and build the intention. Search for the right candle and personalise it some way that is meaningful to you. Take it to the trees, to the flowers, to grass and ask for blessings. Even in the most desolated areas of our biggest cities there will be a tree somewhere, a patch of grass. If this is your circumstance do not be disheartened; nature is always at your elbow and always beckoning. She is present in every breath, every sip of water, every beat of your heart and in every thought.

As I made my way towards Mona I felt as if I was blindfolded, straining to listen, following the tiny rustles and creaks of unseen entities. The nighttime fires became my greatest ally, tiny flaming torches that lit the way. I like to imagine this slender connected thread of small fires insinuating its way into the dark wintery landscape, carving a path from this time to another. A snake lain across the map of Wales, looping and curving its way north with tiny luminescent points of light glowing on its flexing, coiled back. Each time I knelt to light these fires I knelt to the Children's Fire. The repetition was extremely powerful, allowing me to drop deeper and lose myself that I might find a deeper truth. Perhaps word was passed from owl to owl as the fires traced a path to Mona and the dreaming of the Children's Fire. If you make the Children's Fire pledge, then, together with many others, we will illuminate the ignorance within which we have walked for so long. We have learned a great deal in the years between the assault on Mona in 60 CE and our entry into the twenty-first century. Our prodigious gifts do not sit well with childish urges to control and dominate, to place short-term benefits ahead of long-term catastrophe, and to love in such a small-minded, narrow and joyless manner. One tiny fire, then another, then another, hundreds, thousands, millions. Fire can spread with astonishing rapidity. Humans of all ethnic origins, cultures and creeds. It is possible. It is, after all, only a choice, swiftly followed by action. We have a talent for action – it just needs aligning with a purpose that is built on the precepts of love, peace and inclusivity. We could be good at this as well. The chief leaned towards me.

> 'Until the day comes that the people of your islands remember their sacred duty to love and care for the Earth, the Children's Fire will remain extinguished... Until this day comes, we will always be frightened of your people, for you see with dead eyes and your madness may be all it takes to tip the scales.'

> She paused, and then, whispering: 'Mend what was broken. Rekindle the Children's Fire.'

Going Forward

The Children's Fire Programme

In 2019, Mac will be offering an immersive modular programme based around the themes explored in *The Children's Fire*.

The Children's Fire Business Seminar

A short programme for organisations who wish to explore how the principle and practice of the Children's Fire can be introduced, understood and embedded in the hearts, minds and actions of corporations and institutions of all kinds.

Details can be found at:

www.macmacartney.com and www.embercombe.org

Enquiries about speaking, workshops and mentoring

Please contact Mac through his website.

Bibliography

Addison Howard, Helen and McGrath, Dan L. *War Chief Joseph* (Lincoln, University of Nebraska Press, Bison Book, 1964).

Armstrong, Karen. *A History of God* (London, Mandarin Paperbacks, 1996).

Armstrong, Karen. *A Short History of Myth* (London, Canongate, 2006).

Beebe Hill, Ruth. *Hanta Yo* (New York, Doubleday & Company, Inc., 1979).

Berresford Ellis, Peter. *A Brief History of The Druids* (Philadelphia, Pennsylvania, Running Press, 2002).

Caesar, Julius. *The Conquest of Gaul*, translated by S.A. Handford, revised by Jane F. Gardner (Harmondsworth, Penguin Books, 1982).

Collingridge, Vanessa. *Boudica* (London, Ebury Press, 2006).

"hidden treasure" from poet and storyteller Tommy Crawford © 2018 — the right kind of trouble — www.therightkindoftrouble.com.

Elkins, Caroline. *Britain's Gulag: The Brutal End of Empire in Kenya* (London, The Bodley Head, 2014).

Fox, Matthew. *Original Blessing* (Rochester, VT, Bear & Company, 1983).

Goldsworthy, Adrian Keith. *Caesar: Life of a Colossus* (Princeton, NJ, Yale University Press, 2006).

Griffiths, Jay. *Wild* (London, Hamish Hamilton, 2007).

Harari, Yuval Noah. *Sapiens: A Brief History of Humankind* (London, Harvill Secker, 2014).

Hawkes, Jacquetta. *A Land* (New York, Collins, 2012).

Holland, Tom. *Rubicon: The Triumph and Tragedy of the Roman Republic* (London, Abacus, 2004).

Jones, Terry and Ereira, Alan. *Barbarians: An Alternative Roman History* (London, BBC Books, 2007).

Miles, David. *The Tribes of Britain* (Essex, Phoenix, 2006).

Monbiot, George. *Feral: Searching for Enchantments on the Frontiers of Rewilding* (London, Allen Lane, 2013).

Moorhead, Sam and Stuttard, David. *The Romans Who Shaped Britain* (London, Thames & Hudson, 2016).

Parker Pearson, Mike. *Stonehenge: Exploring the Greatest Stone Age Mystery* (New York, Simon & Schuster, 2012).

Piggott, Stuart. *The Druids* (London, Book Club Associates, 1977).

Pryor, Francis. *Home: A Time Traveller's Tales from Britain's Prehistory* (London, Allen Lane, 2014).

Pryor, Francis. *Britain AD: A Quest for Arthur, England and the Anglo-Saxons* (New York, Harper Perennial, 2005).

Pryor, Francis. *Britain BC: Life in Britain and Ireland before the Romans* (New York, Harper Perennial, 2004).

Robb, Graham. *The Ancient Paths: Discovering the Lost Map of Celtic Europe* (London, Picador, 2013).

Schama, Simon. *Landscape & Memory* (New York, Harper Collins, 1995).

Scott, Manda. *Boudica – Dreaming the Eagle* (New York, Bantam Press, 2003).

Scott, Manda. *Boudica – Dreaming the Bull* (New York, Bantam Press, 2004).

Scott, Manda. *Boudica – Dreaming the Hound* (New York, Bantam Press, 2005).

Scott, Manda. *Boudica – Dreaming the Serpent Spear* (New York, Bantam Press, 2006).

Stringer, Chris. *Homo Britannicus: The Incredible Story of Human Life in Britain* (London, Allen Lane, 2006).

Suetonius. *The Twelve Caesars*, translated by Robert Graves, revised by Michael Grant (London, Penguin Classics, 2003).

Tree, Isabella. *Wilding: The Return of Nature to a British Farm* (London, Pan Macmillan, 2018).

Vaughan-Lee, Llewellyn (Ed). *Spiritual Ecology: The Cry of the Earth* (Point Reyes Station, CA, The Golden Sufi Center, 2014).

Waite, John. *Boudica's Last Stand* (Stroud, The History Press, 2011).

Webster, Graham. *Rome Against Caratacus: The Roman Campaigns in Britain AD 48–58* (London, B.T. Batsford, 1981).

Webster, Graham. *Boudica: The British Revolt against Rome AD 60* (London, B.T. Batsford, 1978).

Webster, Graham and Dudley, Donald R. *The Roman Conquest of Britain* (London, B.T. Batsford, 1965).

Williams, Raymond. *People of the Black Mountains* (London, Paladin Grafton Books, 1990).